Update on Christian Counseling

Jay E. Adams

BAKER BOOK HOUSE
Grand Rapids, Michigan

PHOTOLITHOPRINTED BY CUSHING - MALLOY, INC.
ANN ARBOR, MICHIGAN, UNITED STATES OF AMERICA
1980

To My Mother
With Love

Contents

Introduction

Over the years I have discovered myself focusing on certain problems (or aspects of problems) in counseling that I have not treated before. I often speak about these matters at pastors' conferences, and I have written about them in magazines, or have taken notes on studies made for my own benefit, etc.

Now, I have begun to see the need for an open-ended series of volumes, published whenever sufficient material becomes available, that include such emphases. That is why I have published the first volume of *Update on Christian Counseling*. If this course of action commends itself to my Christian readership, I shall continue to do so.

Actually, what should have been the first volume in this series was published under the title, *Matters of Concern for Christian Counselors,** but at that time I had no notion of a series at all. There is another difference between the two books. Articles in this volume are, on the whole, longer than those in *Matters of Concern*.

With this explanation, let us plunge ahead; my goal (as always) is to try to keep the pastor (and other Christian counselors) updated on late developments, ideas, concerns, etc., in the field of Christian Counseling. I hope I shall (in part, at least) begin to achieve that goal through this book.

---

* All of my books that I have cited in the footnotes are available from the publisher of this volume.

I

How Does Counseling Affect the Counselor?

Frequently, in pastors' conferences (I hold a number each year), I am asked the following questions:

> You have done a lot of counseling. When you are talking to people about their problems day after day, how do you keep from becoming unbalanced or morose yourself? And, while you're thinking about that one, how about addressing yourself to this one too—How do you keep from carrying the weight of people's problems away from the counseling room with you?

These are both good questions, and deserve a thoughtful reply. Fortunately, they can be answered together as one combined question to which there is one combined response that covers both. What answers the first question is precisely what answers the second as well. Therefore, I shall treat these questions as one.

Statistical studies show that psychiatrists have the highest suicide rate of all medical professionals.[1] One can understand why. A major reason, I am convinced, is psychiatrists' failure to solve people's problems. When one's profession has as its *raison d'etre* solving other people's problems, and when he doesn't even know how to solve his own, that could be most devastating. Think of the discouragement, doubt and self-accusation that could result. Think of listening to tragic and unsolvable human predicaments, day after day; think of prescribing hopeless and ineffective remedies, few of which bring peace or satisfaction, and many of which seem only to aggravate the

---

1. Cf. *Bulletin of Suicidology* (Washington, D. C.: Government Printing Office, December, 1968), p. 5.

difficulty. No wonder many psychiatrists, daily immersed in human sin and its misery, themselves despair of life itself. Without Christ, what meaning or purpose is there?

So, in answering your questions, I have begun by emphasizing afresh the difficulty you raise. But I have done so in this form to set forth a contrast. The first difference between a truly Christian and a non-Christian counselor is that in Christian counseling the counselor does not offer human solutions (or, as they might more accurately be called, "non-solutions") to human problems. That means (1) they do not rely upon their own persuasions, wisdom and insight; (2) they do not counsel alone. Those who are really engaged in biblical counseling also are involved in the daily use of the Scriptures.[2] *That makes a great difference!* To be reminded of hopeful solutions that *do* work, to share *God's* solutions with others, to actually see the power of the Holy Spirit demonstrated in lives that are transformed in counseling, can be an exhilarating experience! Of course, if under the Christian label, non-Christian counseling is done, that change—because it is a change in name only, and not in fact—will not bring this result. Some Christians, therefore, who ask the question, ask because (like the pagan counselors around them) they know nothing of the joys and victories of the ministry of the Word in counseling.

Many times, after ten hours of counseling, I have returned to my home happier, more excited about the Bible, and actually feeling more rejuvenated than when I began in the morning. Biblical counseling doesn't leave one morose; indeed, it can be one of the greatest encouragements you will ever experience.

"But it can't all be sweetness and light. Aren't there sad times too? Surely, every session isn't exhilarating, is it?"

Of course there are rough sessions, disappointments, heart-breaking events. I had no intention of denying this. I was speaking of the overall impact, the general result—how one is affected by a *ministry* of counseling as a whole.

---

2. For more on this, see my *What About Nouthetic Counseling?*, pp. 41ff.

"Well, then, how do you handle the bad times?"

I'm not avoiding the question; I simply want to look at these matters step by step. Let me say at once that the solution is not the one offered by many who try to assume a "professional" manner, keeping themselves at a distance, never daring to become involved. The idea that I may not feel deeply the hurts and struggles of my counselees is (to me) a totally abhorrent one. Paul spoke of weeping with those who weep and rejoicing with those who rejoice; that is how Christians must minister to one another. So the answer is not in donning the white coat and assuming an air of clinical objectivity.

"But, how does the counselor avoid carrying more burdens than he can bear?"

Certainly not by becoming aloof. Many people think that the sort of involvement Paul described as "weeping" and "rejoicing *with*" surely would lead to utter despair. That's why they try to keep their distance. They are very wrong. It is the person whose emotions are not spent in the counseling session who finds them troubling him later on. While I am not advising counselors to lose control of their emotions (Paul didn't intend that either), it is necessary to enter into the counselee's problem as fully as one can; that means in thought and emotion—yet without losing perspective. The counselor's proper stance is empathetic disagreement (not empathetic agreement).[3] On this stance, he appreciates every feature of the counselee's problem as fully as he can; he tries to understand all dimensions, *in depth.* But—and this is *critical*—he refuses to see the problem only as the counselee does. If the counselee declares, "My situation is hopeless," he replies, "No, you are wrong; although the situation is *very* serious,[4] it *isn't* hopeless. God has an answer even to this. . . ." Because the counselee *knows* that there have been true understanding and empathy *in depth,* he cannot dismiss the coun-

---

3. For a fuller development of this concept, see my *Lectures on Counseling,* pp. 85ff.

4. He never minimizes the problem; in the spirit of Rom. 5:20b, he maximizes the Savior.

selor's disagreement. (If the counselor remained "professionally" aloof, the counselee might readily wonder whether he truly understands.)

The counselor, then, acknowledges the problem for all that it is. (At times, he will even point out other aspects of the problem that the counselee has missed and that make it even more serious than he supposed: "You see, this isn't only a matter of your relationship to your wife; it is also a question of your relationship to God.") But the counselor is never problem-oriented. Having adequately ascertained the true nature of the counselee's difficulty (and even when analyzing it), he offers hope from God. That is to say, his basic stance throughout is redemptive—he is solution-oriented. Always—from the outset—he holds forth the truth that God has answers, even to a problem like this. Non-Christian counselors cannot do this; they have no such stance.

Empathetic disagreement makes a great difference. He is empathetic (he doesn't downgrade the difficulty), but he always disagrees with the counselee who sees his situation as hopeless. Instead, his focus is upon biblical solutions. He believes that there is hope (forget everything, if you don't) and, in all he says and does, he conveys it. Counselors who have no such hope to offer doubtless become as discouraged as their clients. Often they advise divorces (for example) because they can see no other (better) way out. They know nothing of God's solutions to marital problems and can offer no hope. No wonder they carry a shoulder-full of burdens around.

So, summing up what we have discovered so far, we have seen:

1. The Christian counselor has the exciting and satisfying advantage of doing counseling in which he can see the results of the Holy Spirit transforming lives through the ministry of His Word.[5]

2. He has hope to offer.[6]

---

5. Incidentally, biblical counselors everywhere testify to the joy and satisfaction that they find in this ministry.

6. For an exhaustive study on hope (its importance, place and source), see pertinent passages in my *Christian Counselor's Manual.*

3. He is solution-oriented, not problem-oriented. (Some psychiatrists must content themselves with the dubious task of affixing a label to the person or his problem.)

"But what, now, of his failures, and the failures of his counselee? They don't all come through this with flying colors. What about those heartbreaking incidents you mentioned earlier? You haven't dealt fully with my questions yet."

O.K., we're now ready to move on. The Christian counselor knows from the outset that both he and his counselee are far from perfection. But he also knows that God is perfect. So, he counsels not from his own imperfection but from the stance of God's trustworthiness and power. That is, he points always to hope in God (never to himself). From start to finish the hope that he holds out is found in the Scriptures, where God has gone on record about life and the solutions to the problems posed by sin (cf. Rom. 15:4, 13—hope comes from God through His Word).

Because of this basic stance, the counselor himself can take seriously the advice that he gives his counselee about worry (cf. Matt. 6; Phil. 4).[7] Having worked hard at ministering God's Word to a counselee in any given session (and biblical counseling is *hard work*[8]), prayerfully, at the close of the session, he commits the counselee and the outcome of the session into God's hands and *leaves the matter there.* He has been doing the Lord's work; the Lord will watch over its results. Then and there he turns his mind to the next counselee (or whatever other responsibility that he has at hand). He *refuses* to carry problems home because to do so would be sin— he asked God to carry the burden; how, then, can he take it back from Him? Worry will do no good. He can do nothing more than what he has done; but God can. In the final analysis, you see, it boils down once again to *faith*—does he *believe* that God cares and will act? Worry is connected intimately to unbelief. But if he believes

---

7. See my pamphlet, *What to Do About Worry*, for a fuller explication of these verses.

8. I have discussed this matter in *What About Nouthetic Counseling?*, pp. 59ff.

that God will work through His Word *in* counseling sessions, why shouldn't he believe also that God will continue to work when the session is over? In a sense, what he believes about his counseling in general (God is/isn't at work in it) makes all the difference about his attitude between sessions. The answer, then, is not to stand aloof, or develop an insensitive and callous attitude or anything of the sort. The answer is trust—trust in God's promises both within and outside the counseling session.

Now, one other factor of importance should be mentioned to assure balance in what I have said. The counselor must make sure that he has given all that he can of himself in the counseling hour; this is vital. He must begin counseling prayerfully, asking God's help (after preparing for it thoroughly), and during the hour-long session must concentrate all his efforts on determining (in biblical terms and categories, according to scriptural values) what the problem is and what God says must be done about it. He must work hard at developing creative and concrete applications of biblical principles that are appropriate to the circumstances peculiar to each case. He doesn't confine his approach to rubber-stamp solutions, which are supposed to fit all cases (see the chapter in this volume on "Adaptability in Counseling"). Now, when he has done all this, he knows that he has done all God expects of him—so, why worry?

However, he will fail. When he does—and recognizes it—he confesses this to God and to the counselee. He knows, and has made it clear to the counselee in one way or another (usually by stressing hope in God, not in himself), that he isn't perfect. That is why it is essential to orient all hope toward God and the promises of His Word. There is little wonder that psychiatrists who must counsel exclusively by human power and wisdom often come to despair. The counselee's hope and faith is placed in *them*. Not so with the Christian counselor; while he is to prove himself eminently trustworthy, nevertheless, at times he will fail. Therefore, he directs the counselee to place all his trust in the unfailing Creator and Sustainer of the universe. God can succeed, even when the counselor fails.

There is one more matter worth raising. All biblical counselors

6

know that there is usually a point where things get worse before they get better. Counselors unfamiliar with this phenomenon often give up (or allow their counselees to give up) when this happens. Nathan had his rough session with David before the daylight of Psalm 51 flooded in! Do not despair, therefore, when difficult sessions occur. Indeed, wise counselors sometimes warn, ahead of time, of the likelihood of such an experience:

"There are going to be some difficult things God will require of you. You may feel worse before you feel better (like when you go to the dentist, or have an operation). Sinful patterns are stubborn and do not budge easily. At times, when they finally come loose, it is painful; there may be bloodshed. But don't despair—this is the darkness before dawn; this is the valley of the shadow of death that leads to the green pastures and still waters."

So, you see, biblical counselors expect difficult sessions and are not thrown for a loss when they have them. It is all part of a day's work in counseling!

"But what if a counselee messes everything up, or quits counseling—or, commits suicide?"

No one likes to think about these things, but we must, of course. I have had counselees go the wrong way in spite of the hope God offers; I have never (yet) had any commit suicide. But I have had to think about that possibility.

Jesus knew what it was like to have counselees quit. The rich young ruler walked away. And Judas committed suicide. So the problems are not unique; they have been faced before, and handled rightly by Jesus Himself. Obviously, Jesus didn't go all to pieces, or give up. He showed sorrow for the young man, but in both cases He clearly *placed the responsibility where it belonged*—on the young man and on Judas.

Jesus, Himself, did not fail. The failure belonged to the one who turned away. And *that is how Jesus viewed the situation*. The play was a success; the audience was a failure.

It is the counselor's obligation, as God's steward, to minister (or dispense) the Word accurately and faithfully (I Cor. 4:1, 2); it is

7

the counselee's responsibility to obey the Word. The counselor can explain the Word, encourage the counselee to obey it, warn him of the consequences of disobedience, but he *cannot make him obey.* If the counselor has discharged *his* responsibility, then he is clear. How the counselee responds is *his* responsibility, and his alone. If the counselor has failed in one way or another to assume his responsibility in the relationship, that makes him responsible (not for the counselee's failure but) to repent, to seek forgiveness and to rectify his failure as he is able to do so. The counselor *never* bears responsibility for the counselee's actions; the counselee *alone* bears such responsibility. The two responsibilities must be sorted out. Even if the counselor fails (he's responsible for that), the counselee is responsible for making a proper response to that failure. If he gives up on God, or even commits suicide, the counselor must not hold himself responsible for that. Poor counseling, though tragic, is not an adequate justification for the counselee to do either of these things in response. The counselee bears full responsibility for his sinful response, just as the counselor must for his sinful failures.

While the two responsibilities are separate, they are related. Any true counselor would deeply regret any failures on his part that the counselee used as an occasion to turn from God or to commit suicide. Yet it is wrong for the counselor to bear the guilt of the counselee's action. He has enough guilt of his own to deal with. Sin by one person neither causes, nor justifies, nor necessarily occasions sin by another. Because there is so much confusion abroad in society today, it is important to recognize this truth, and to understand Jesus' approach to the problem.

All in all, then, the Christian counselor takes a biblical stance, and has an approach to counseling that is coupled with hope and powerful resources that keep him from becoming unbalanced about life, or morose. He finds that if he is a hard-working person who assumes his obligations both in counseling and at home, he will not have time to sit and brood and become morose. He doesn't carry problems home. When he fails, and does carry problems around, he has no one to blame but himself. In that case, he must do some reorienting of his counseling schedules, procedures, attitudes, stance (or whatever else may be at fault) to become more biblical. He will find that he must apply to himself some of the principles that he uses in counseling (especially those relating to self-pity and worry). And, in the event that this doesn't help, he may find it helpful to chat with other Christian counselors who have overcome the problem.

2

Failure in Counseling

I have mentioned this phenomenon before,[1] but it seems necessary to say more about it in some depth.

"I agree with you entirely about avoiding a feeling-orientation in counseling, and I know that I must not allow counselees to say 'can't' if they are Christians, but listen Jay, aren't there still some persons who really *can't* do some of the things they say they ought to do?" Such were the words of a faithful pastor who has been trained in nouthetic counseling and who has been successfully using it in a fruitful ministry. Because his problem is not an isolated one, it ought to be addressed.

In the vast majority of the sort of cases that he had described, the answer (I told him) is not that the counselee *can't* do what he knows he should, but that he *won't*. In spite of clear-cut, concrete assignments, willingness to help on the part of the counselor and others, and a desire by the counselee to be helped and to follow scriptural counsel, in the end counseling fails because *the counselee persists in following counsel in his own way*.

When asked, "Did you do what I said?" he will invariably reply, "Yes, I did; but it didn't work." He isn't always sincere in this answer, but often he may be in spite of the fact that the reply is misleading and actually is a distortion of the truth. His own patterns of selectivity may be so dominant that, without explicitly focusing upon the fact of what he is doing, he may really hear only that part of a

---

1. *The Christian Counselor's Manual*, pp. 233ff., 245ff., 459-461.

counseling assignment that he wants to hear.[2] So, as a consequence, he winds up doing only a part of what he has been told, doing it in a different way from the way that he was advised, or substituting something apparently similar but essentially different from[3] what he was counseled to do.

There are people who (when advised to get a product), always end up purchasing a substitute; and usually they find it unsatisfactory.[4] For instance, a mechanic says that a Toyota oil filter will handle the oil better than any substitute can (and warns that the latter could lead to a $200-plus motor job if the owner persists in replacing the filter with a cheaper substitute). The owner hears (the problem is not selectivity), but he isn't sure, indeed, doesn't *want* to believe, or tells himself, "That's what they all say; he just wants to make a buck." He is a fool not to take such advice (or at least to carefully check it out before rejecting it) and run the risk of ruining his motor. Yet, there are any number of people who do just that because that is their pattern of thinking. In a sinful world where people do lie, and as sinners themselves, they have adopted this attitude. Then, when they come to God's Word, the same attitude is carried over. For one rationalized "reason" or another—there are any number of possibilities here—the basic perversity of sinners manifests itself by saying, "I know better; I don't really have to do *that* (or do it *that* way)." Then, when things fail (as inevitably they do), they blame the person whose counsel they did not follow. They complain that his advice was inadequate, conveniently omitting the fact that they failed to take it!

Physicians are acutely aware of the problem. A physician told a woman with high blood pressure, Hodgkin's disease, and a number of other related problems, "Don't drink coffee." She said in my

---

2. There is evidence that sense data can be re-routed around the brain. Unless the reticular formation arouses one to attend, data can be missed.

3. See the chapter in this book, "Don't Apologize!" Frequently, when told to seek forgiveness, counselees will substitute apology instead. But, as that chapter makes clear, the two are essentially distinct. See also, *infra.*

4. I say usually, because (in such matters) it is possible to stumble upon something equally as good or better. But any substitute for God's ways, in the end, will *always* fail (although at times it takes a while to discover this).

presence, "My husband said that a cup or so every morning won't hurt me." She complains about her condition continually, but she won't follow the doctor's directions. Physicians, who are aware of and concerned about this perverse, sinful tendency of patients not to follow directions, do three things that it also might be helpful for counselors to do:

1. They spell out directions very clearly. A counselor ought to do the same, writing out assignments in detail and going over them with his counselees. At points he will find it necessary to add words like these—DO EXACTLY WHAT THIS SAYS! NO DEVIATIONS.

2. They check up on the patient to make sure that their directions were followed. Counselors who give assignments, but fail to check up on how they were carried out, are kidding themselves (usually the early part of each session is devoted to checking out homework *in detail:* "Tell me, step by step, what you did and what happened").

3. They warn (like the Toyota mechanic) about the possible serious consequences of failing to follow directions. The Bible motivates by positive and negative means: promise and warning (cf. my discussion of this in *Matters of Concern,* pp. 28-31).

Now, let's take an example. Suppose you have told a counselee to ask God for forgiveness for a particular sin and then go to the person he has wronged by it and seek his (or her) forgiveness as well. The counselee agrees. All looks well. When he returns for the next session, he reports that he has done so. (You fail to check out the exact particulars of what he said and did.) Pleased, you go on to other matters. Then, at the next session, the counselee announces that "this business of seeking a brother's forgiveness hasn't done any good." Things, he indicates, aren't any better; in fact, they seem worse. He says, "I'm sorry I took your advice."

There can, of course, be many other dimensions to such a problem (failure on the part of the offended party to forgive, or to live up to his promise of forgiveness. But, for the sake of simplicity in making the point, let's leave these possibilities aside for this discussion[5]). But let us say that this is what happened:

Your counselee heard your advice. However, he "translated" your words (even when written, this can happen), "ask forgiveness" into "make up with" or "tell him you're sorry" or "apologize." That isn't what you *said,* and it isn't what you *intended,* but it is what (in his sinful perversity) he *did.*

What he did was *partial.* He went to the offended party as you directed, but it was also *perverted:* he did something qualitatively different. He did not follow directions. He said, "I'm sorry," instead of "I've sinned; will you forgive me?"

Now, there could be any number of reasons why he fulfilled the assignment in this way. Take two:

(1) It could be his pattern to "do things his own way."

(2) He could genuinely not have known the difference.

Let us consider (2) more closely.

In this case, the counselor also bears some responsibility. Counselors ought to know about such perversions of biblical action; they should know that people substitute apologies for seeking forgiveness. And, therefore, they should spell out exactly what asking for forgiveness entails. In fact, they should anticipate such a possible "translation" and guard against it by clearly distinguishing the two things when giving the assignment. Because so few persons recognize the difference, and because most people persist in confounding forgiveness and apology, of necessity good counseling involves spelling out *in detail* what is and (with equal clarity) what is *not* meant by the assignment. And, it would be well to warn against substituting the one for the other. He might explain,

"Seeking forgiveness and saying 'I'm sorry' are two entirely different ways to handle the same situation. One is God's way; the other man's substitute. The former stems from repentance (leading to confession—an admission of sin—and to the granting of pardon); the other may stem from sorrow (often, as in Esau's case, men-

---

5. But not, however, in a genuine counseling context if the other party can be brought into the counseling session as well.

tioned in Hebrews 12:15-17, sorrow arises over the *consequences* of sin, rather than the fact of sin as an offense against God and others, and his inability to reverse them). The two differ radically. An apology is no more than a statement about one's feelings: 'I'm sorry.' It is non-specific—is he sorry about what happened to himself or to others? Does he recognize the fact that he has sinned, first and foremost against God? What do the words mean?

"Because they are non-specific, the words of apology elicit some non-commital response (if any is forthcoming at all). Why shouldn't they? They are vague, and (indeed) ask for no commitment from him. Having made an apology, one may *assume* that the matter is closed. The truth is that it is not. Neither party has committed himself to closing the question; nothing has been done about the past act or about their future relationship. This leaves all options open.

"In contrast, asking for forgiveness is quite specific, when done biblically. Say to the one you wronged, 'I have sinned against God and against you [Luke 15:18]. I have confessed my sin to God [if you have], and I know He has forgiven me; now I ask you to do the same. Will you?' Such a statement is specific. By it you recognize the serious nature of what you have done—it is sin, against both God and him. Secondly, it asks for a concrete response on the part of the one that you wronged (don't settle for a non-committal reply like 'Forget it.' Say, 'No, this was sin. That requires forgiveness. I want to set the matter to rest; will you forgive me?'

"Sometimes the person wronged is willing to settle for less so that he can go on holding the offense against you. If he dodges an answer, or refuses to forgive, remind him of Luke 17:3-10. If he still refuses, Matthew 18:15ff. comes into play (with another believer).[6] He must say either 'yes' or 'no.' You must know the answer.

---

6. In seeking forgiveness from an unbeliever follow Rom. 12:18 (for a thorough discussion of this, see my book, *How to Overcome Evil*).

14

"When you go to another, the object isn't merely to express your feelings—even of regret. You must go (as the Scriptures make clear) to be reconciled to him. The substitute, 'I'm sorry,' does nothing about the *relationship;* the biblical way opens the door on a new beginning.

"And, one more thing—if either you or the person to whom you go doesn't understand what forgiveness is, and, therefore, what the granting of forgiveness entails, let me tell you plainly. Then you can explain to him what you have in mind. Forgiveness is a *promise.* When God forgave you in Christ, He promised not to 'remember your sins and iniquities against you any more.' The one who asks for forgiveness also asks for *that;* the one granting forgiveness promises *that*—and nothing less. This promise is threefold in his case:
  (1) 'I won't bring the matter up to you again'
  (2) 'I won't bring it up to others'
  (3) 'I won't bring it up to myself' (i.e., allow myself to sit and brood over it in self-pity).

Asking and granting forgiveness implies future effort to work for a new, biblical relationship. When God reconciled us to Himself, He didn't leave the matter with forgiveness. Once the sin was forgiven, He insisted on building a new, proper relationship with us (cf. Eph. 4:17).[7] Now, what do you think of this? Is it clear? Do you have any questions?"

Some such presentation of the assignment must be given (whatever the subject may be). By going into it in some detail (you may even want to *read* this to a counselee at times) you will forestall all sorts of problems. By giving an opportunity for feedback at the close, often you can discover whether the counselee understands, believes, intends to follow directions, etc. His response usually will lead to further clarification of the issues.

In spite of such specific directions, warnings, etc., some counselees

---

7. On this, see my *Matters of Concern*, pp. 36ff., where I discuss how reconciliation must lead to a new relationship.

15

will persist in "doing it their own way" with the usual consequences. When they come to you complaining about the need for a $200-plus repair job on their relationship, they must be told—in no uncertain terms—who failed.[8] How do you do this?

Fundamentally, there is but one thing to do (a variety of approaches may be used, however): gather complete, exact data about what the counselee did/said and did not do/say. Many counselors settle for arguing about incomplete, inexact data; they do not probe deeply for facts. After all, if what you told him truly is biblical (and now we assume it was), then the counselee is charging that God has failed, that His Word isn't trustworthy. This is serious and cannot be handled like an egg, "once over, lightly."

Ask questions: "How long did you do it? What was the tone of your voice when you said that?" etc. You may have to say, "Tell me specifically, in detail, step by step, what you did and said; what he did and said in response. First, you went to him—where? Under what circumstances? Were others present? Did you make an appointment? . . ." and so it must go (on and on at times). When you require facts, you will soon discover what is at the bottom of his failure. More often than not—as you might expect—there it is, an ersatz oil filter!

When you get hold of that filter, you can show him plainly—explain what went wrong and begin to deal with what, perhaps, is an equally serious (or even more serious) problem—this pattern of doing things another way.

Well, I've told you. I've advised you to do several things. But I am certain that some of you—even you Christian counselors—will say, "Well, yeah, maybe so . . . but I think there's another way to do it."

---

8. Of course, if the counselor also failed in any way—perhaps in not becoming specific enough—he should confess this and seek forgiveness from the counselee, thus becoming a model for him.

3

Stress—A Christian Approach

Let's talk a bit about stress. Since Hans Selye's studies, stress has been in the news. What do Christians have to say about the issue? The word is used in several ways by various people to denote different things. Therefore, it is essential, at the outset, to define the term as I shall be using it in this chapter.

Popularly, the word stress is used as a synonym for what I shall call *pressure*. By pressure I mean force exerted upon an individual's body (or some part of it). This force may be located either without or within the individual himself. In this chapter I shall not use the word stress in that sense. Whenever referring to such force, I shall always use the word *pressure*.

More technically, the word *stress* refers to debilitating bodily responses to these inner and outer pressures. It is a response in which various normal bodily reactions are (1) maintained for too long a period of time, and/or (2) heightened to a more-than-optimal level. Stress, then, refers to any harmful, self-induced strain upon the body or upon various parts of or organs in it.

I have distinguished between these two terms in order to set forth the biblical viewpoint on stress and pressure more clearly. Some such distinction (use whatever terms you prefer) is necessary in order not to confound things that the Bible separates (as some, in speaking of this subject, have done). Pressures from without (or even at times from within) may not be avoidable; stress (since it is part of an inner, learned response) always is.

It is most important for counselors to recognize this point. If stress is (as many think) unavoidable, then three things follow:

1. The individual undergoing stress is not responsible for it.
2. He is a victim of what others (or circumstances) have done to him.
3. In most instances he can do nothing to alleviate it.[1]

Moreover, it is not at all helpful to speak of *stressors* (as if persons could automatically turn on stress in another by their presence, words or actions). Neither persons nor situations can do anything of the sort. They may *exert pressure,* but not *cause stress.* To speak of stressful situations is, therefore, equally bad. Stress, like tension, is in *persons;* not in circumstances. It is fine for authors and poets to rhapsodize about tension "in the air" or "between" people, but it is wrong for counselors to do so. Tension is always in muscles. Stress is always an electro-chemical response in a person that (like tension) is subject to his control by (1) developing and making biblical interpretation and (2) responses to persons or situations that exert pressure. According to some theorists, stressors are persons who always elicit a stress response in the counselee. While it is true that such a response may *regularly* occur, the reason lies in the counselee himself, not in the so-called stressor. The word stressor ought, therefore, to be scrapped because attention ought to be focused primarily on the changeable habitual response pattern of the counselee, and only secondarily upon the source of pressure.

That fact is significant because it indicates that the counselee, far from being a helpless victim, controlled by the whims of others and the winds of circumstances, is responsible for the stress that he (alone) places upon his body.

Stress, then, is the result of habitual, sinful responses. In counseling it is important to make this clear to counselees. They must be given hope by recognizing that stress is sin. Jesus Christ came to deal with

---

1. I wish to make it clear that I am not including bodily injury or illness, which may cause bodily strain (one system breaking down can place great pressure on another), in this analysis. Sometimes nothing *can* be done about such bodily strain because medical science has no answer to it.

sin. By the Spirit's power, working through His Word, these responses can be exchanged for non-stressful, biblical ones. And the counselee must be held responsible for availing himself of all God's resources for doing so. Stress, as I have defined it, then, is the counselee's own sinful, body-harming response to pressure.

Thus far I have spoken almost entirely of outer pressures. There are inner pressures too. These are *generated* within the counselee by the counselee himself. A sense of guilt arising from unconfessed, unforgiven sin may lead to bad bodily feelings triggered by conscience (the capacity for self-evaluation according to a value standard). Anger, worry and fear (for the wrong reasons, in the wrong intensity, unrelieved by the proper biblical resolution of matters) are others.

In one sense, almost all outer pressures also are inner. Outer pressures do not truly become such (unless they are physical) until (or unless) they are *interpreted* by the counselee as pressures. If a sneer is taken as a smile of approval, it is not very likely to be taken as an occasion for a stressful response. Often, seeing events more biblically, trusting God for his explanation of them, or learning that there is a proper biblical response to them, alleviates the pressure. The outer non-physical event itself really has no power to elicit a stress response. Another's sin cannot make me sin. I won't respond that way unless I am willing to do so. Otherwise, Jesus Himself would have sinned; it would have been inevitable. He would have sinfully injured His body by sinful stress reactions. The fact is—as we know—He did not. We confuse the issue because we look at sinners (even redeemed ones) who so often do respond sinfully—then declare that a pressure ➤ stress response is inevitable. Referring to Jesus makes the distinction I have maintained crystal clear.

Regardless of where the pressure that brings a necessity for response originates—within or without—the counselee must not be viewed as a helpless victim, trapped in its web. The Scriptures teach the counselee how he is to interpret and respond to trials, persecution and other hard times as a Christian. They explain what he is to do about guilt. If he injures his body by responses that set loose harmful chemical and muscular states, that is his fault. If he had fol-

19

lowed the Bible, stress wouldn't have occurred. He cannot blame stress on pressure; ultimately, to do so is to blame God, Who sovereignly controls both circumstances and persons.

Now, it is unnecessary for the counselee to understand fully how resentment (e.g.) leads to colitis for him to stop putting stress upon his colon. All he needs to know is that the Bible forbids resentment and that it charts another course of action for the Christian in the handling of his anger (cf. Eph. 4:26-32,[2] where the believer is told not to let the sun go down on his anger, and where he is told how to respond by building the other up with his words, while he destroys the problem that has arisen). If he follows this and other biblical directives pertaining to anger and the responses to other pressure-type situations, stress will not occur.

Whether or not the counselor elects to explain something of the physiological dynamic involved, he must always make it plain that (in the end) the *major* reason for avoiding resentment is *not to avoid stress,* but to please God by obedience. That is why a simple believer, who lives in a manner pleasing to God, can live a stress-free life, purely by studying and following the Bible (cf. Ps. 119:98-100). The one who makes glorifying God his constant goal truly finds that he does *enjoy* Him as well!

Surely the Apostle Paul (not to speak of Jesus Himself) was under unbelievable pressures (cf. II Cor. 4:8, 9, 16, 17; 6:4-10; 11:23-29). Those passages, if they indicate anything, show that he should have had colitis, ulcer, heart problems, etc., if the current pressure = stress view were true. Yet, he had none of these difficulties because even though undergoing greater pressures than any counselee you will encounter, he did not subject his body to stress through sinful interpretations and responses to these pressures. That is why he could go on serving Christ under such trial. Like Christ, Who did not get ulcers on the cross because He prayed for those who were condemning Him to death, Paul handled wrongdoing toward himself rightly (cf. Phil. 1, etc.).

---

2. See *The Christian Counselor's Manual* for more on this.

Paul's case vividly illustrates the falsity of the modern view symbolized by the simple equation

$$\text{Pressure} \longrightarrow \text{Stress}$$

This is too simplistic a view. A true biblical picture looks like this:

$$\text{Pressure} + \text{sinful response} \longrightarrow \text{Stress}$$
$$\text{Pressure} + \text{righteous response} \longrightarrow \text{Peace}$$

The difference between the two constructions is the difference between responsibility and irresponsibility, the difference between hope and despair, the difference between health and sickness. Christian counselors will be well advised to maintain a sharp distinction.

4

Drugs and Counseling

Of course there are other types of medicine (e.g., medicines to fight infection, inflammation, etc.); but I'm not thinking about those in this chapter. Rather, what I have in mind are the two types of drugs given to persons who are involved in the sort of behavioral problems that also lead to counseling. Questions often are raised by counselees about these. Counselors must grapple with the effects of drugs on counselees, and (in general) there are a number of reasons why a Christian counselor ought to take a clear-cut position about them.

Probably the most convenient way for laymen to think about such drugs is to divide them into two categories. These are:

1. Drugs that supplement bodily chemicals.
2. Drugs that inhibit bodily functions.

Drugs of the first category, like insulin, do for the body what it ought to do for itself, but (for one reason or another) doesn't. They meet *a genuine bodily lack,* a need. Such drugs do not interfere with normal bodily functions, but assist them and make them possible.

Drugs of the second category include the tranquilizers and other drugs that are given to *inhibit* certain normal bodily functions. In other words, *these drugs have an opposite purpose and function.* The use of such drugs is

1. Highly questionable in most instances.
2. If appropriate at all, only for a very brief, temporary period (e.g., to calm a counselee in a suicidal or hysterical state).
3. Never to be used when counseling ought to be given instead;

cannot be substituted for changes of behavior that ought to be effected by the Spirit of God through the ministry of His Word.

These rough guidelines may be of help to Christian counselors who (in a variety of situations) may have to deal with such questions. While counselors may not prescribe drugs, they may

1. Refuse to counsel when they find that because of its side effects they are talking to the pill more than to the person.
2. Call the prescribing physician (with the counselee's permission) and request that the drug be eliminated.
3. Encourage the counselee to assume more personal responsibility for behavior change, and urge him to face rather than run from problems (into drugs), leading to speedy disuse of drugs of the second sort.

Drugs of the second category often create new problems for those who take them, some of which are equally as serious (from the counselor's viewpoint) as the problem they are designed to relieve. Actually, they do not solve problems; they only mask them.

For helpful, further suggestions, each pastor should develop a close working alliance with a physician who recognizes the importance of not over-prescribing drugs. From this alliance may come various benefits, one of which will be a better understanding of drugs that it is impossible to include in this broad summary.

5

The Practicality of the Sermon on the Mount

One fact that I have insisted on over the years (and have worked hard to rectify) is that conservative churches have been strong on the *what-to* (in both preaching and counseling—i.e., where they have done biblical counseling at all), but weak on the *how-to*.

I

In counseling I have discovered that many counselees are in serious trouble because, while they know *what* the Lord requires of them, they do not know *how* to go about meeting these requirements—no one ever told them. Indeed, many don't even know where to begin. Again and again in counseling sessions the breakthrough comes when I begin to apply known scriptural truths practically (concretely directing the counselee in the ways and means of kneading biblical principles into the dough of his life). That's when he comes alive and things begin to happen. Before, he knew what to do (at least generally, though sometimes this needs sharpening too); this he had been taught again and again (in Sunday School, from the pulpit, in Christian books). And usually I find that he has tried, only to fail again and again. Soon (characteristically) he gives up, saying, "Well, maybe Paul can do it, but I'm not Paul." This failure syndrome is widespread in the church.

The answer to the problem—as I have taught in all my books—is to begin to include the *how-to* in all counseling. When I caught on to this and began to focus on this in my counseling practice, I also began to see a tremendous difference in counseling results. If my past 14 years of counseling experience has demonstrated anything, it has pointed out the utter need for creative practicality in the *use* of the Scriptures.

Now, as I said, I have hammered away at this point, given many examples of what I mean and have taught others also how to use the Scriptures practically (that doesn't exclude exegesis and theology, but rather seeks to achieve individual applications of both). But, as I scan my books, I notice that I have largely *assumed* that this was a biblical emphasis; I have not adequately supported that assumption from the Scriptures themselves. And, in question-and-answer periods this has been pointed out by various questions from time to time. So here I shall make one initial thrust that—in and of itself (I believe)— should establish this practice as biblical.

If, over the years, any unit of biblical material has been thought of as "idealistic" or "impractical" by those who do not believe or do not understand (or are unsympathetic with) its teachings, it has been the Sermon on the Mount. I propose, therefore, to examine this sermon (as it appears in the Gospel according to Matthew) to show (1) that the charge of impractical idealism cannot be sustained and (2) that the Scriptures clearly demonstrate that (in His preaching) Jesus was concerned equally with the *what-to* and the *how-to*. The Sermon on the Mount, I think you will agree (when I am through), is eminently practical. Moreover, along the way, I hope to discover some of the how-to for the development and use of how-to. So let us begin.

II

The first section of the Sermon on the Mount (Matt. 5:1-20) is introductory; it sets the stage for what follows. One would not expect much application in the introduction to a sermon. The beatitudes (which have very practical implications for life—someone has quipped, "The beatitudes are the attitudes we ought to be at"—but these are not spelled out practically) give an exciting profile of what God's people may (indeed *must*) become. Here, in this list, are both their ideals and their hope. Then, in summarizing the influence

25

that Christians like this may bear, Jesus says they must be salt (a preserving influence) and light (an illuminating, guiding influence). All these ideals are possible and may be realized, not by overthrowing the O.T. principles of living (vv. 17-19) but (unlike the scribes and Pharisees) by properly interpreting, applying and living according to those commandments in all their fulness (v. 20). This fulness would be described by Jesus in the sermon that follows and demonstrated by Him in the life He would live and the death He would die.

The phrase, "You have heard . . . but I say," refers not to the O.T. Scriptures—as though Jesus were abrogating God's principles of living taught there—but to the false scribal interpretations *and applications* (He takes up *both*[1] and, therefore, counters *both* with correct alternatives.) In the sections that follow, Jesus shows how to *interpret* and to *apply* the Scriptures properly. Naturally, He makes concrete, practical, *how-to* type applications in doing so. Even the conclusion to the sermon fits this analysis; it too is practical in emphasis: The Christian's righteousness will exceed the righteousness of the scribes and Pharisees when he learns *both* to *hear* and to *do* all Jesus commands.

N.B., Jesus lays emphasis upon *both* hearing and doing; He sees no place for truth unapplied and unappropriated. The what-to is not enough (in some ways, that was the Pharisee's problem: he knew the what-to, but he either failed to work it out in daily living, or did so in a perverted way); it must issue in practical Christian living.

Following the introduction, Jesus becomes practical and specific. First He takes up the sixth commandment, the one that prohibits murder (v. 21). The scribes had restricted its application to the limited circumstance of actual homicide. But Jesus makes it clear that the commandment is broad; He shows too that it has an inner application as well. Therefore, it includes unrighteous anger, and the expression of such anger in words. For instance, two Christians must never allow any matter to separate them because of anger.

---

1. Most commentators have stressed the interpretations alone. The two can be distinguished but, of course, cannot be separated; the one supported the other.

Bitterness and resentment may not come between them; they must be reconciled.

"But what happens when, in this world of sin, they do allow such things to come between them?" someone might ask. Jesus anticipates the situation, and (in very practical *how-to*—here even step-by-step—terms) He tells us *how to* handle the situation (vv. 23, 24). The practical how-to comes in the form of a procedure growing out of the priority of reconciliation. Clearly verses 23 and 24 are how-to verses.[2]

Next, Jesus makes a second application of the sixth commandment. Once again He shows exactly how it may be applied, this time, when dealing with an unbeliever. In a pending court trial, it is better not to let your anger keep you from doing the sensible thing—settling out of court, as quickly as possible. Otherwise, you may be sorry.

So, as Jesus discusses the sixth commandment, we note that He offers two case studies and recommends specific, concrete action, often in the form of steps ("First . . . then"). These are important principles for counselors to understand and follow.

But that is just the beginning. Next, He turns to the seventh commandment (vv. 27-30). Again, after broadening the commandment beyond the mere outward act to include the heart, He turns to how-to (vv. 29, 30). If one must not look on a woman lustfully, then (the question arises) *how* can he avoid doing so? He gives a concrete answer: by putting impediments in his way. Whatever member of the body has been offending (even a *right* eye, *right* hand, *right* foot——*right,* indicating the most important), it must be removed. Jesus never intended this to be understood literally. His point was, as mutilation would make it difficult to perform an act again, so whatever led to adultery (or any other sin) of the heart similarly must be removed. The truly repentant believer does not want to offend again, so (and this is the *how-to*) he will do all he can to make it difficult to fall into the same sin again.[3]

---

2. Cf. Matt. 18:15ff.; Luke 17:3ff. for other step-by-step how-to directions about the same matter.

3. For more on this, in detail, see my *Christian Counselor's Manual,* ch. 19.

In verses 31 and 32, Jesus takes up another false interpretation that (again) leads to sinful action. Deuteronomy 24 was not intended to allow or institute divorce, but only to regulate it. In this case, the Pharisees had broadened a narrow O.T. passage to make it teach things that it was not designed to say. So, Jesus narrowed it once again to the correct interpretation (I cannot treat the many ramifications of the divorce/remarriage question here. I have tapes[4] available on the question and am writing a book on the subject). In the process, Christ clarifies the biblical position on divorce, the exception to it (among believers) and the results of violating the biblical position by misusing the Scriptures for one's own purposes. There is no *how-to* here, because the discussion is (essentially) negative; but there is plenty of how *not* to!

Turning to the next passage (vv. 33-37), Jesus tightens up another commandment that was being misused by the Jews. Their preoccupation was with the exact formula of oath-taking. By cleverly worded vows and oaths they could seem to swear when they didn't do so at all—or at least that's what *they* thought! Christ was concerned about honesty—being a man of one's word. One's reputation for honesty should be so stainless that his word alone is sufficient (he need not swear).[5] But the important fact, for our purposes, is the clear-cut how-to that Jesus gives. He teaches explicitly that one must solve the question of oaths *beforehand,* not afterward (v. 37—He must always mean yes when he says "yes" and no when he says "no"). Christians must stop playing word games altogether (vv. 34ff.). Simply, clearly, say yes or no and mean it. That is long-term, sweeping, but explicit how-to. It sliced through all the confusion, arguments and sophistry. No casuistry was needed.

In verse 38, another issue is raised. The Christian's personal ethic must be distinguished from civil punishment (Paul picks up on this

---

4. Available from Christian Study Services, 1790 E. Willow Grove Ave., Laverock, Pa. 19118.
5. On this passage (and the entire sermon) see John R. Stott's excellent book, *The Christian Counter Culture* (Downer's Grove, Ill.: InterVarsity Press, 1978).

in Romans 12 and 13). As individuals, we must learn to respond with love, overcoming evil with good (for a full discussion of this see my *How to Overcome Evil*). Verses 39-42 are *how-to* verses—each explains *how* God wants Christians to handle pressure and persecution rather than retaliate. To help, again Jesus illustrates the how-to principles by cases that clearly might apply to actual situations that any one of them might face.

In verses 43-48, Jesus continues this basic theme: a Christian must *love* his enemies. But, unlike many modern preachers, Christ didn't leave the concept of love hanging in thin air—undefined and amorphous. Rather, He was quite specific: love focuses on the other person; not on one's self. Therefore (note the specific how-to) a Christian must pray for his enemies. That concrete proposal Paul developed (as we must develop all such suggestions) in Romans 12:14ff.

And so the sermon continues. There is no let-up on the practicality of the material confronted in chapter 6. Here, the general principle is set forth: Don't do righteousness for the approval of others, or that is *all* you will get for your efforts. Jesus cites four areas of abuse (note how He works a principle into a number of practical situations):

1. Giving charity for personal acclaim (vv. 2-4);
2. Praying like the hypocrites (vv. 5, 6);
3. Praying like the pagans (vv. 7-15);
4. Fasting to exhibit humility to others (vv. 16-18).

To each of these four areas, Jesus appends some how-to advice that (if followed) will keep the Christian from falling into the traps just mentioned. Here it is:

Verse 3—Do your giving anonymously.

Verse 6—Pray regularly in a private place.

Verses 9-13—Pray briefly and to the point, listing distinct items in sequence, ridding prayer of all unnecessary repetition.

Verses 17, 18—Fasting before God alone.

Indeed, as you can see, even the so-called Lord's prayer was given (at this place) in order to show *how to* pray (cf. v. 9a). It is a how-to model.

The next section of the sermon (vv. 22-34) covers the interrelated sins of avarice and anxiety. The answer to avoiding these Siamese twins is stated in very practical terms (vv. 33, 34):

1. Set your priorities properly (v. 33);
2. Focus your efforts and concern on solving today's (not tomorrow's) problems (v. 34).[6]

Chapter 7 continues along the same lines. What to do about judging is the theme of the first five verses in this chapter. Jesus not only sounds a warning against sinful forms of judging, but He lays out a concrete how-to procedure that (1) will prevent one from sinful judging and (2) will help him to judge righteously (v. 5). In modern terms, the how-to principle may be stated this way: Put the lid on your own garbage can before complaining about the odor from someone else's.

Though this discussion has been brief and summary, I think it is perfectly clear by this point that Christ was concerned about how-to as well as what-to. Without detailing the rest, notice how-to instructions (continuing throughout chapter 7) in verse 7 (ask if you want something), verse 12 (treat others as you'd want them to treat you), and verse 16 (you can discover false prophets by observing the fruit of their teaching in lives—theirs and those of their disciples). Then, to cap off the whole sermon, Jesus insists on *doing* what He has said, not merely hearing it. But to know how is not the same as to show how. Jesus recognized this, and throughout the sermon insisted on *showing* how.

Now, in conclusion, let's draw together a few principles that will help us to understand *how to* use *how-to*.

1. Jesus gave specific instances of what He taught; He used case studies. He didn't merely state principles abstractly as so many do today. You can actually picture (in your mind's eye) the

---

6. Verse 34 has been unpacked in a pamphlet, *What to Do About Worry*; verse 33 could (likewise) be treated much more fully.

man laying down his gift on the altar, getting up, leaving, looking for his brother, etc.

2. Jesus illustrated principles so they would be clear and memorable. Once having heard it, who could ever forget the splinter and the board of Matthew 7, or the principle it illustrates?

3. When giving a specific case (plucking out the eye that adulterously looks on a woman in lust), Jesus generalized (to the hand, and elsewhere to the foot) as well. He thereby extended the principle of making it difficult for one to sin again to all sorts of situations.

4. Jesus even gave actual models to follow (cf. the Lord's prayer).

Let us be thankful for the practicality of the Sermon on the Mount. Jesus showed us the importance of such practicality in Christian instruction. We too, in the ministry of the Word (in preaching and in counseling), must do the same.

6

Don't Apologize!

It is time to say it clearly—so that no one may misunderstand: the Bible nowhere advises or allows (and certainly doesn't command) apology.

Yet, in spite of this fact, Christians (and even Christian counselors) somehow seem to be addicted to apologizing and advising counselees to "go apologize" to others whom they have wronged. To all such, I have one piece of advice: Stop it!

"Well, what on earth is wrong with apologies?"

Fundamentally, two things.

I

An apology is an inadequate, humanistic substitute for the real thing. Nowhere do the Scriptures require, or even encourage, apologizing. To say "I'm sorry" is a human dodge for doing what God has commanded. And (as we shall see) since it is man's substitute for God's requirement (and has all but replaced that requirement), it has caused a great number of problems in the church. By replacing the biblical requirement for dealing with estrangement, it has allowed estrangement in the church to continue unchecked.

"What is this biblical requirement that has been replaced?"

Forgiveness.

"Forgiveness?"

Yes. I shall not now develop this point by discussing the numerous passages that speak of Christian forgiveness. Instead, I shall simply refer you to other treaments of the subject.[1]

---

1. See *The Christian Counselor's Manual,* pp. 63-70, 88, 361; *Christian Living in the Home,* ch. 3.

As long as Christians continue to say to those they have wronged, "I'm sorry" (or words to this effect), instead of "I sinned; will you forgive me?" and as long as they receive the natural response, "Oh, that's all right" (or something similar), the real solutions to the many difficulties that could have been reached through forgiveness will continue to be by-passed. The church will labor under the burden of resentments and bitterness on the part of its members.

"Why do you say that?" you may wonder. Let me explain; and that explanation leads to a second point—apology is wrong, not only because it is man's inadequate substitute for God's revealed method of righting sour interpersonal relationships, but (as such),

II

apology elicits an inadequate response. When one asks, "Will you forgive me?" he has punted; the ball has changed hands, and a response is now required of the one addressed. The onus of responsibility has shifted from the one who did the wrong to the one who was wronged. Both parties, therefore, are required to put the matter in the past. And, the proper response (Luke 17:3) is, "Yes, I will." Like God's forgiveness ("Your sins and iniquities I will remember against you no more"), human forgiveness is a *promise* that is *made* and *kept*.

When one person says, "I forgive you," to another, he promises:
1. "I'll not bring this matter up to you again"
2. "I'll not bring it up to others"
3. "I'll not bring it up to myself (i.e., dwell on it in my mind) "

The response, "Yes, I'll forgive you," then, is a promise that entails quite a commitment—one to which the forgiven brother (and God) may hold him, and one that (if kept) will lead to forgetting the wrong (not forgive and forget, but forgive to forget) and re-establishing a new, good relationship between the parties involved. So, an apology is an inadequate substitute because (a) it asks for no such commitment, and (b) gets none.

An apology keeps the ball in one's own possession. The other party is required to do nothing about it (and usually doesn't). To

33

say "I'm sorry" is, you see, nothing more than an expression of one's own feelings. To say, "I have wronged you," and then to ask, "Will you forgive me?" is quite another thing.

Therefore, counselors (in advising counselees[2]) must be quite clear about this matter. When they are, and when a proper understanding of this matter once again begins to permeate the Christian church, many of the current difficulties we are experiencing will disappear. Let's do our part in hastening that day.

---

2. See an earlier, spelled-out explanation of how to do this in the article entitled, "Failure in Counseling."

7

Presuppositions and Counseling

All counseling systems rest upon presuppositions. For instance, Freudianism (as one among many assumptions) presupposes that human beings are the product of evolutionary development. It also presupposes that human beings behave as they do because of their unconscious. Rogerianism presupposes that (at the core of his being) man is basically good. It also presupposes that he is filled with untapped potential and solutions to all sorts of problems. Skinnerianism presupposes that man is nothing more than an animal. It also presupposes that by changing the contingencies in his environment, man's behavior can be manipulated. These are only a few of the presuppositions (or basic ideas) that govern and condition all the research (it is *not* objective), practices and development of methods and techniques within these systems. Everything in a consistently framed system grows out of and depends upon its presuppositions.

So does biblical counseling depend upon its presuppositions.

In order to think about this matter more clearly, I have listed (not exhaustively, but suggestively, in random order) what (in my opinion) are some of the presuppositions that are foundational to biblical counseling. Read carefully the 25 presuppositions that follow and see if you agree with them.

1. There is such a thing as peculiarly *Christian* counseling.
2. Not all counseling done by Christians is Christian counseling.
3. The Bible is the sufficient source for the principles needed to do Christian counseling.

4. God is the sovereign Creator and Sustainer of the universe.
5. Counseling depends ultimately upon the work of God's Spirit.
6. Man was created in God's image as a responsible being.
7. Human thought and behavior is moral.
8. Man is a sinful being, guilty and corrupt as the result of the fall.
9. Man's corrupt nature leads to sinful behavior and behavior patterns.
10. Sin results in misery.
11. Unregenerate persons cannot be changed by counseling in a way that pleases God.
12. Regeneration by the Spirit is a prerequisite for biblical change and obedience.
13. Problems of regenerate persons can be solved God's way by God's power.
14. God requires and equips His officers ín the church to counsel as a life calling.
15. God requires and equips all believers to counsel.
16. The church must become involved in counseling.
17. Church discipline is an important factor in biblical counseling.
18. Methodology must grow out of biblical principles and practices.
19. Non-Christian content or methods may not be eclectically incorporated into a Christian system.
20. Counselors should expect and see results from Christian counseling.
21. Counselors must study the Scriptures telically.
22. True counseling is a ministry of the Word leading to sancti- fication.
23. Unbelievers must be evangelized before they can be counseled.
24. Problems with an organic base also should be handled medically.
25. The Scriptures set forth the principles for human living that were demonstrated in the life of Christ.

Now, as I said, this list of presuppositions is not exhaustive (indeed,

I arbitrarily cut off the list at the number 25 so that it would not become unmanageable). But every presupposition is important.

Something of the importance of holding correct presuppositions, and of avoiding falseness, is plainly pointed out by Paul in Galatians 4:9:

> But now that you know God (or rather, that you are known by God), how can you turn back to those weak and pitiful presuppositions? Do you want to be enslaved by them once again?[1] (The New Testament in Everyday English).

Here Paul makes it clear that false presuppositions enslave. One's thinking and actions grow out of his presuppositions, as we have seen. He is bound to his presuppositions. How important, then, it is to have biblical presuppositions on which to found one's life and life work! Whoever is "bound" to God's presuppositions is free indeed.

Some (perhaps many) who read will have little or no difficulty with all (or most) of the 25 presuppositions. Others will find snags all along the way. If you are among the latter, I urge you to study the Scriptures carefully to see whether these things are so (but as you do so, carefully examine the presuppositions that you bring to my list and to the Scriptures).

Presuppositions are of great importance (as I said) because they govern all that we do in counseling (as elsewhere). Therefore, it is important to become aware of our presuppositions. Reading the list may help you to do so. Perhaps you would find it helpful to write up your own list of 25 presuppositions to contrast, amplify or supplement mine. At any rate, becoming aware of presuppositions is vital to any serious thought and practice in counseling.

---

1. Hendriksen's arguments for the interpretation of *stoichea* as basic (or elementary) principles (= presuppositions) are convincing. The references to angels or elementary spirits are all late and specialized.

8
Getting Organized

Recently, in speaking with a pastor who is unsuccessfully attempting to counsel a couple who have separated (and who give clear evidence of many irregularities and erratic tendencies in their lives) I was struck afresh by the fact that many (perhaps most) pastors do not structure their counseling adequately. Clearly, as our conversation continued, it became apparent that much of his failure stems from this lack.

Instead of setting formal times and places for counseling on a regular basis, I find that many pastors counsel in a very spotty way—whenever they happen to think of it, whenever there is pressure to do so, whenever they are faced with some pending calamity or whenever the spirit (not the Spirit) moves them. And, they will counsel anywhere, whether the conditions are optimal or not (even when there is no emergency to do so).

No wonder, then, that all too few counselees are helped by this hit-or-miss approach. Often, biblical counseling gets a bad press from this sloppy imitation of it. Such shoddy counseling procedures are deplorable (just as bad as carelessly prepared sermons) and must be corrected. Pastor, if these hard words apply to you—then it is time for you to get organized!

Most counselees (whatever their other difficulties may be) need discipline in many areas of their lives. Even if lack of discipline is not the central problem, accompanying it is the need for order, regularity and persistence—in short, order and discipline. Without it, other problems cannot be solved; order and discipline are preconditions for successful counseling. When the counselor not only fails to demand discipline of his counselees, but also fails to structure orderly conditions for change and, himself, lacks discipline, he thereby inhibits and impedes, rather than furthers, his counseling goals. His own modeling can defeat all that he says.

Why are order and regularity important? Because, among other things, no counseling (as I said) can take place where disorder and confusion prevail. In attempting to put off old sinful behavior patterns and put on new ones, discipline is of the essence (see my booklet, *Godliness through Discipline;* cf. II Tim. 4:7). Two of the basic elements of discipline are order and regularity. Success in replacing old patterns with biblical ones greatly depends upon these two elements. The counseling climate and structure must provide for discipline.

Man was made in God's image. God is "not a God of confusion"; He is a God of orderliness (cf. I Cor. 14:33). On the basis of that fact, Paul ordered the Corinthian church to do everything "decently and in order." But the principle that, because He is not a God of confusion, He demands order, is broader than the worship context to which it was applied. The principle itself is stated without such limit; it has a place in all the work we try to do for Him. He will not have us in confusion in His Name.

To reflect God's ways in our activities, we must be willing to be orderly in *our* affairs. God planned His work, then worked His plan. Christ came "in the fulness of time"—i.e., right on schedule. He often said words like, "My hour hasn't yet come"; when it did, He noted that fact too. He was conducting His ministry according to a divine timetable. Orderly sequence, planning and scheduling obviously are all elements of the amazing ministry of Christ. Our ministries too must reflect these qualities.

Now, of course (in necessity, on occasions of rare opportunity, etc.) one could counsel anywhere, at any time—we have often said, "We could counsel on a subway." At one point I had to use my VW Microbus as a counseling office. There also must be flexibility (*our* programming isn't divine!); our schedules must not be chiseled in stone. But surely to depart from a well-thought-through schedule ought to be the exception, not the rule. Unfortunately, in some cases, the opposite is true.

When a counselor's approach to counseling, then, is spotty, unstructured, irregular and doesn't follow a prayerfully constructed schedule, he simply shouldn't expect consistently good results. Indeed (unwittingly) he is programming his counseling, even though he doesn't know it—for failure. You cannot overcome the disorderly patterns of others' lives by more of the same. If you have problems saying "no," refusing to counsel under less than optimal conditions (when they are available), etc., read my suggestions about these matters in *Matters of Concern,* pp. 83, 84.

I suggest, therefore, that you chalk out certain hours for counseling. They can be largely afternoon hours. (Men take off from work to see other counselors, physicians, dentists, lawyers, etc.; they will do the same for you.[1] What you offer is a service equally as important as any of these, to say the least.) Then, set up weekly sessions for each counseling case. (A full course of life occurs every seven days. About that much time, therefore, is needed to work biblical principles and practices discussed in the session into all aspects of life.)

So, pastor, let me ask you—have your counseling practices been orderly? If not, then it is time for you to get organized, don't you think?

---

1. Regularly, pastors complain, "I don't charge money like a counseling center does, so my people aren't as motivated as theirs." That is wrong. Time *is* money. Proper appreciation for time (yours and the counselee's) can solve all such problems. Why should your family be penalized by your absence every evening for counseling to accommodate others merely so they can make more money. Think through *everyone's* priorities, including your own; be sure they are God's.

9

Using the P.D.I.

In nouthetic counseling circles, the P.D.I. (Personal Data Inventory) has been used for some ten years or more (a copy is reproduced at the end of this article). During that time, it has proven very helpful. Its use has been explained to those who have studied at C.C.E.F. and at the training centers in this country that are associated with N.A.N.C.[1] But many other persons who have become involved in biblical counseling also have become familiar with it. As a result, from time to time, I have been asked to explain its use. I shall do so in this article. N.A.N.C. training centers may find it very helpful to assign the reading of this article to new trainees. First, I shall say a few general words about the P.D.I., then I shall simply move through the form, in order, commenting on various uses and the possible interpretations of responses in each.

First, then, let me suggest that you *always* use a P.D.I. in *every* counseling case. You may ask, "Do you really think I should? For instance, should I have every member of my congregation fill one out? I already know all these things about them." The answer is yes and no. Probably you will do well to have page 3 (the pink page) filled out by *everyone*. But, in such cases, it would be well for *you* (as pastor) to fill in all the data you can on the first two (yellow) pages, from your own records and personal knowledge. As you do, you

---

1. CCEF = The Christian Counseling and Educational Foundation, 1790 E. Willow Grove Ave., Laverock, Pa. 19118 (P.D.I. forms may be purchased at this address). NANC = The National Association of Nouthetic Counselors, 100 Doncaster Dr., Lafayette, Ind. 47905.

will discover that *in most cases* you actually have far less information than at first you may have supposed. Try it; you'll be astounded that you were going to counsel with so little knowledge about essential data. I think, therefore, it won't be long before you will begin to use the P.D.I. with everyone—including your members.

In instances where you begin to counsel persons totally unknown to you, you will discover that the P.D.I. uncovers much valuable data quickly. I recommend that you use it more frequently and more fully than (at first) you may be inclined to.[2]

Who fills out the P.D.I.? In most cases, the counselee should arrive at least a half hour prior to the first counseling session. The church secretary then hands the P.D.I. to the counselee(s)—one to each counselee—and tells him (them) to fill it out. When this has been accomplished, the secretary brings the completed form(s) to the pastor, who goes over it privately. Five minutes of consideration of the form by the pastor ought to prepare him for the interview.

The counselor makes notes (question marks, checks, underlines, exclamation points, etc.) on the P.D.I. as he considers it (the P.D.I. is his property, and he retains it, along with weekly records and other data, in his manila file on the counselee). Usually, notes are made with a red felt-tip pen so that, when needed, he can spot these readily in the sessions that follow. At the top of page 1, if there is a husband and wife, he marks down a large "H" or "W." This enables him to quickly note which P.D.I. belongs to which counselee. Because he must often locate material quickly during discussions that follow, such notations really help. Sometimes he also copies notes from the P.D.I. onto the agenda column of the W.C.R. (Weekly Counseling Record[3]).

Items that the counselor marks on the P.D.I. (or places in the

---

2. Sometimes the easiest way to ask a counselee a potentially embarrassing question (especially a member of your church) is through a written form (obviously, a printed sheet was not designed particularly for some one individual). Some of these questions might never be asked (or the data gathered) otherwise. Use of the form indicates concern for thoroughness; most members appreciate that.

3. Available also at address given in footnote 1, *supra*.

W.C.R.) are quite varied. They may include such matters as, "Why did the Dr. prescribe that drug?" "Check out this emotional upset," "Should I phone the physician about this?" "This sounds important," "Vague," "What was the reason for the arrest?" etc. Usually, the counselor will work out his own abbreviations for such notes (e.g., "Why drg?" "Phys?" "Imp?" "?" "reason?"). The notations that he makes will form the basis for further inquiry and discussion.

Now, let us look at the P.D.I. itself.

Under *Identification Data,* everything is rather straightforward. If any of the data are omitted, check these omissions with a red pen and (early in the first session) find out why. In *some* cases *failure to include data* (here or elsewhere) *could be significant.* Ask later about it.

Clearly, check marks by the counselee in the separated or divorced blanks call attention to themselves immediately. Underline them, and discuss these matters early in counseling (especially when the dates given are quite recent). Other checks in the widowed, single, going steady blanks could be of importance (and may figure significantly at a later point), but *usually* don't call for immediate discussion.

Answers to the questions concerning *education* can be informative. If, for instance, the wife is a college graduate and the husband didn't complete high school, one *possible* source of difficulty (to be explored) immediately comes to mind. If, in addition to other parallel data, you discover that the counselee dropped out of high school in his senior year, that fact may be profitable to investigate. It could indicate the first evidence of a life pattern of quitting when the going gets tough.

Information on who referred the counselee also can be helpful in any number of ways. Perhaps this person himself can help. At some point you may wish to ask the counselee's permission to invite this party to a session to disclose certain data. You may wish to call him/her during a session for information about some point, or to seek his/her assistance in a project that the counselee may undertake in his homework.

These uses of identification data are only suggestions, of

course, but they serve to show you how much you can learn from seemingly "standard" information. Begin to discover for yourself how much more is revealed by such simple responses.

Now, let us turn to *Health Information*. Obviously, answers that indicate that the counselee's health is declining (or those substituted under "other") require investigation. Large losses (or gains) in weight may indicate either physical problems or significant emotional turmoil. Past illnesses (e.g., a coma), handicaps (e.g., a club foot), or injuries (e.g., a concussion) can be of significance in understanding a counselee's problem. Pursue carefully any that *may* seem to link up. Send for medical reports, phone a physician for an evaluation, etc. CCEF starter kits for counselors[4] contain a *Release of Information Form* that the counselees may sign to obtain data from a physician. The simplest way to get this is to ask the counselee to ask his physician to send you a report.

The date of the counselee's last medical examination can be important. Reports of recent examinations are often *very* helpful. Be sure to send the counselee for an examination when you feel there is any possibility that there is organic dysfunction behind certain behaviors, unless he has just been examined *for the problem under consideration* and the report is negative (be sure you *see* the report; for various reasons, counselees may misread, misunderstand or, at times, falsify reports).

Naturally any mood-changing drugs that the counselee is taking may be of importance to counseling. You may be talking to the pill rather than to the person if you are not careful about this question. A normal response (apart from drugs) may be brighter, exhibiting more concern, or less anxiety. See the chapter in this volume, "Drugs and Counseling" for further information (or my larger chapter on drugs in *The Big Umbrella*, where I have tried to set forth some guidelines for helping persons who depend on drugs).

You will want to obtain last year's P.D.R. (Physician's Desk Reference) from your physician so that you can look up the effects of

---

4. Available at the Laverock address.

drugs on your counselees. Side effects of some drugs affect counselees quite dramatically. There have been times when counselors have noted these and have had the counselee notify the prescribing physician about the fact.

The question about "severe emotional upsets" often elicits very important data. Investigate the data very closely. Frequently, the counselee will indicate events (or patterns) here that can lead quickly to the heart of some difficulty. Pursue the data given here fully enough to discover the nature of these upsets and whether they recur according to some pattern.

A *yes* response to the question on arrest (which seems out of place here, but isn't—we get honest answers by including it here) can be of significance. By asking "When?" you (as I once did) may receive this retort, "My wife had me locked up last week." Clearly, this reply has put you onto something right away.

There is little that I need to say about the *Religious Background* section; to Christian counselors, the value of such data is great. The *exact* wording used is important because it is designed to cover (and uncover) all sorts of facts from all sorts of persons. A *tentative* evaluation of the counselee's faith and life may be gained by a careful reading of his responses. But this evaluation should never be absolutized; it must be subject to re-evaluation at any time. The last question about "recent changes" often brings out important facts. Learn to ask for further details regarding answers given here.

We now turn to page 2 and *Personality Information.* The first two questions about previous counseling are *very* important. If the counselee indicates that he has had counseling before, you will want to know (1) with whom and to what extent, (2) whether failures have destroyed his hope (look especially for this where he has been to many counselors),[5] and whether his mind has been filled with erroneous concepts and/or excuses derived from previous counseling

---

5. If this is the case, see *The Manual* (on hope) for how to generate hope again.

45

(listen for psychiatric or psychological jargon in his descriptions of his problem). *In all cases,* try to discover:

(1) What was attempted or done in previous counseling (sometimes new problems grow from counseling).

(2) What the counselee was taught (and believed) about himself, his problems, others, life, etc.

(3) What the counselee did about any advice that he was given.

(4) What the outcome was.

(5) What the counselee's present evaluation of previous counseling is.

From a *discussion* of these data, you will often learn much about a counselee himself, as well as something about his life problems. Don't miss either angle.

The words to underline and circle help you to discover the present (note the word "now") state of the counselee. If she circles nervous, impulsive, moody, often-blue, introvert, self-conscious, lonely, sensitive, you can almost count on meeting a depressed woman (or one on the depression skids, traveling fast) in a few minutes when she comes through your door. The same circles, however, may (in fewer instances) indicate heavy medication, grief, etc. I will not try to open up all of the possibilities that various combinations of marked words *may* indicate (note: always read these answers in relationship to others in the P.D.I.). Instead, I suggest that you try out the list on yourself, your friends and counselees. From their responses, and what you know of them, begin discovering which combinations *usually* (not always) indicate what. You will want to develop your own reference chart. You'll learn more from this than if I were to tell you how various combinations may indicate certain trends (and you'll enjoy doing so). One last note on this section—Answers to "other . . . ." will be infrequent. Ones given usually are highly significant.

The next series of questions, extending from, "Have you ever felt people were watching you?" to "Do you have problems sleeping?" are there to uncover possible perceptual problems. A series of yes answers, particularly yes answers about hallucinations and sleep loss, may be of great importance. Some persons seem to suffer from perceptual problems due to drugs, sleep loss or chemical imbalances and malfunctions within their systems. Effects upon perception (seeing, hearing, smelling, tasting, touching, perceiving depth) may occur in almost any combination and intensity. The counselor should look for

(1) Multiple responses (sleep loss and hallucinations, etc.). If there are a number of such problems, he has stronger reason to suspect perceptual difficulty.

(2) Misunderstood responses (an attractive woman may have problems with people watching her—not from perceptual difficulty but because of her beauty.

Perceptual problems can cause great difficulty; it is hard to live with them. Yet some causes are quickly remedied by (1) sleep, (2) removing toxic substances from the environment, (3) massive vitamin therapy, etc. In cases where there seems to be difficulty unrelated to drugs or sleep loss, a further question-and-answer test may be used to confirm or deny the suspicions that grow out of these sample questions. This is the H.O.D. (or Hoffer-Osmond diagnostic test) mentioned in *Competent to Counsel*, pages 37ff.

Turning now to *Marriage and Family Information*, we discover that the P.D.I. asks what seems to be largely routine, clear-cut questions. That is true, but there are some uses of answers that may not immediately be as apparent as the questions that evoked them. Let me mention a couple of these (you'll soon discover others) to give you some idea of what I have in mind.

Occupations, for instance, often are areas of concern and pressure (gobbling up a husband's time, difficulties at work brought home, misery from failure to find an occupation that matches one's gifts, working at a job that one's spouse disapproves, etc.).

The response that a couple has filed for a divorce or has been separated on previous occasions, shows immediately that there has been long-standing difficulty in the marriage. Many of those former problems will have never been solved. Troubles may be complex and quite complicated by now (cf. *Matters of Concern*, p. 20, for help in sorting things out). Find out the occasions for those previous difficulties, what they led to and how they are related to the present problem (directly—"same old thing again"; indirectly—"before it was his mother; now *he's* acting just like her").

When the wife's age is greater than her husband's (especially if there is a large gap), it is possible (but not *necessarily* so) that she married him as a last resort. Look for bitterness and resentment in either or both parties. Very short engagements *may* indicate poor reasons for marriage in the first place (explore this); or very long engagements *may* indicate indecision, or other problems.

Many children, spaced closely together, *in some cases* also may cause problems—look for resentment. Previous marriages (especially investigate the thorny problem of integrating children from them—occasions when this has been done well are rare) often cause difficulty. Wrong patterns, expectations, fears, and odious comparisons, developed in a former marriage may (unnecessarily) be carried over to the present one. Indeed, it is likely that this has happened (look into it).

Where the counselee was in the lineup of siblings (how many older/younger brothers/sisters he had) often has significance ("Dad had nothing for me, but after I left home his financial picture improved and the other kids cashed in; I resent it").

Now, we turn to the pink sheet (the colors are mildly motivational). The five questions here allow the counselee to tell his/her own story in his/her own way. No one could structure beforehand all the questions that might cover all situations that occur among counselees. Hence this page (it also allows for some duplication that invites comparison with previous answers. Significant contradictions should be probed).

In these answers, you may learn a lot not only from the data given but also from *how* it is given. Does the language—grammar, vocabulary and sentence structure—indicate good or poor communicative skill? Wisdom? Foolishness? Poor communication skills often point to misunderstandings, etc. Circle (in red) nasty, harsh words (to be referred to later when discussing communication). Other attitudes often emerge too (hesitation, over-qualification, etc.). In answer to questions 1-3 a teenager wrote:

Q. 1.—What is your problem?
A.—Nothing.
Q. 2.—What have you done about it?
A.—Nothing.
Q. 3.—What do you want me to do about it?
A.—Same thing.

At least two facts were apparent:

1. He didn't want to be there and had no hope;
2. He had a sense of humor (note the switch in answer to no. 3). It was through humor that he was reached, and eventually given hope and helped.

When two or more parties come for counseling, it is interesting to compare and contrast the answers that they give to questions 1-3. Some obvious problems emerge instantly when you see quite diverse understandings of the same difficulty (or its causes). That, itself, may be *one* problem (or the *basic* one at times).

The answer to question 1 tells you how the counselee sees his difficulty, and on what level (symptomatic or causal). The precision (or the lack of precision) with which he describes it also can be revealing. If he knows and can state clearly what his problem is (and is not deceiving himself), then you need not waste time trying to discover it or explain it. (Be sure his understanding is correct—find out how he arrived at this interpretation. Confidence and clarity don't always flow from correctness.) If the counselee's words are fuzzy (on the other hand), you will have to help him sharpen his focus. The difficulty may lie in his ability to express himself, in his understanding of his problem, or in both of these areas. Check out *both*.

After all supplementary information about answers on the first sheet has been gathered by orally asking questions growing out of written responses, the best place to begin talking is with question 1. I usually read it out loud (for him and any other counselee present) and then say, " Can you tell me something more about. . . ." or "When

49

did you first discover. . . ." or some similar question that grows out of the written response.

I have discussed this before,[6] but let me here remind you briefly that answers to question 1 can be given on any one of three levels:

1. The level of *irritation*. This is what irritated the counselee or others (or both) enough to motivate him to come (e.g., "I've been depressed for over three weeks"). Of course, his interpretation (what he *took* an event, or series of events, to mean or be) may be wrong. Indeed, his interpretation of the problem may be correct, partially correct or wrong (e.g., he may see an event as a crisis, even though it isn't.[7] But so long as he perceives it to be so, he will react to it in that way). People who settle for solving problems at the irritation level often care only for (symptomatic) relief. Such persons usually settle for drugs, etc.

2. The level of the *causal event*. Here, you read answers like, "I was fired from my job for lying." The counselee may see this as the basic problem, when (actually) it may be the culminating result of other, more basic problems. Don't settle for this if there is more. On the other hand, don't invent problems that don't exist.

3. The level of the *underlying* pattern. The particular causal event ("I blew up at her") may be but the latest in a long series of such outbursts under similar circumstances. To seek forgiveness, therefore, is proper but inadequate. The counselee's habitual response pattern itself must be exchanged for a biblical one. Otherwise, the problem will continue to crop up in the future. Much more could be said about question 1, but probably that is enough to remind the regular reader of nouthetic counseling books about the things that have been said elsewhere.

Question 2 yields much helpful information. Look especially for:

a. Right things done in wrong ways.

---

6. The *Manual*, pp. 274ff.
7. *Lectures*, pp. 107ff., where imaginary crises are discussed.

b. Wrong things done, thought to be right.

c. Right things partially done.

d. Complicating problems, growing out of previous wrong actions.

e. Continuing erroneous efforts.

Usually, the discovery of complicating problems is the most valuable fact that you will have to uncover in answer to this question. With that I shall leave it.

Question 3 is important. This *agenda* question lets the counselor know (1) whether he and the counselee have the same objectives. When they differ, agendas must be renegotiated until they both agree— with the Scriptures ("It isn't enough to want your wife back, Joe; you must want to change because God says so—whether Phyllis returns or not"); (2) whether the counselee has hope (if not, you must help him to generate biblical hope—cf. *The Manual* on hope). Without understanding these facts, counselors often will spin their wheels, getting nowhere, and failing to understand why.

Question 4, in itself, usually is fairly unproductive, but sometimes may yield interesting information. In comparing and contrasting the answers here with the words circled on the previous page, you may discover interesting inconsistencies that are profitable to explore (don't try to do all this right away, however; put such items on your agenda for later). Usually, the way that one sees himself *basically* (not necessarily as he is *now*) will be described in this question.

Because no questionnaire can foresee all situations, question 5 has been included. Often very valuable data will be picked up by this question. Always *pay close attention to* whatever is included in this answer. More often than not, it contains clues (sign pointers) to the basic problem.

Hopefully, this discussion of the P.D.I. will be useful in encouraging its use (leading to more productive counseling), and its *proper* use. Careful, thoughtful study of answers to the questions on the P.D.I. may speed up counseling by getting to the heart of issues from the outset. The P.D.I. cannot do everything; do not depend solely upon it. But for whatever value it may have, may it help you to be a more faithful counselor for the Lord Jesus Christ.

PERSONAL DATA INVENTORY

IDENTIFICATION DATA:

Name _____ Phone _____

Address _____

Occupation _____ Bus. Phone _____

Sex _____ Birth Date _____ Age _____

Marital Status: Single_____ Going Steady_____ Married_____

Separated_____ Divorced_____ Widowed_____

Education (last year completed): _____ (grade)

Other training (list type and years) _____

_____

Referred here by _____

Address _____

HEALTH INFORMATION:

Rate your health (check): Very Good___ Good___ Average___

Declining___ Other___

Weight changes recently: Lost_____ Gained_____

List all important present or past illnesses or injuries or handicaps:

_____

_____

Date of last medical examination _____

Report: _____

_____

Your physician _____

Address _____

Are you presently taking medication? Yes_____ No_____

What _____

Have you ever been arrested? Yes_____ No_____

State circumstances: _____

_____

Are you willing to sign a release of information form so that your counselor may write for social, psychiatric, or medical report? Yes_____ No_____

RELIGIOUS BACKGROUND:

Denominational preference: _____

Member _____

Church attendance per month (circle):   0   1   2   3   4   5   6
7   8   9   10+   Baptized? Yes_____ No_____

Church attended in childhood _____

Religious background of spouse (if married) _____

Do you consider yourself a religious person? Yes_____ No_____
Uncertain_____

Do you believe in God? Yes_____ No_____ Uncertain_____

Do you pray to God? Never_____ Occasionally_____ Often_____

Are you saved? Yes_____ No_____ Not sure what you mean_____

How frequently do you read the Bible? Never_____ Occasionally_____
Often_____ Do you have regular family devotions? Yes_____ No_____

Explain recent changes in your religious life, if any _____
_____

MARRIAGE AND FAMILY INFORMATION:

Name of spouse _____

Address _____

Phone _____ Occupation _____

Business phone _____ Your spouse's age _____

Education (in years)_____ Religion _____

Is spouse willing to come for counseling? Yes_____ No_____
Uncertain_____ Have you ever been separated? Yes_____ No_____
When? from_____ to_____

Has either of you ever filed for divorce? Yes_____ No_____
When? _____

Date of marriage ————————————————————

Your ages when married: Husband———— Wife————

How long did you know your spouse before marriage? ————

Length of steady dating with spouse ——————————

Length of engagement ————————————————

Give brief information about any previous marriages: ————

————————————————————————————————

Information about children:

PM*	Name	Age	Sex	Living Yes No	Education in years	Marital status

*Check this column if child is by previous marriage

If you were reared by anyone other than your parents, briefly explain:

————————————————————————————————

How many older brothers———— sisters———— do you have?

How many younger brothers———— sisters———— do you have?

Have there been any deaths in the family during the last year?

Yes———— No———— Who and when: ——————————

————————————————————————————————

PERSONALITY INFORMATION:

Have you used drugs for other than medical purposes?

Yes———— No———— What? ——————————————

Have you ever had a severe emotional upset? Yes———— No————

Explain ————————————————————————

————————————————————————————————

Have you ever had any psychotherapy or counseling before?
Yes_____ No_____ If yes, list counselor or therapist and dates:

_____

_____

_____

What was the outcome? _____

_____

Circle any of the following words that best describe you now:
active ambitious self-confident persistent nervous hardworking
impatient impulsive moody often-blue excitable imaginative
calm serious easy-going shy good-natured introvert extrovert
likable leader quiet hard-boiled submissive self-conscious
lonely sensitive other _____

Have you ever felt people were watching you? Yes_____ No_____
Do people's faces ever seem distorted? Yes_____ No_____
Do you ever have difficulty distinguishing faces? Yes_____ No_____
Do colors ever seem too bright? _____ Too dull? _____
Are you sometimes unable to judge distance? Yes_____ No_____
Have you ever had hallucinations? Yes_____ No_____
Is your hearing exceptionally good? Yes_____ No_____
Do you have problems sleeping? Yes_____ No_____
How many hours of sleep do you average each night? _____

BRIEFLY ANSWER THE FOLLOWING QUESTIONS:

1. What is your problem? (What brings you here?)

2. What have you done about it?

3. What do you want us to do? (What are your expectations in coming here?)

4. What brings you here at this time?

5. Is there any other information we should know?

10

Flexibility in Counseling

One of the problems that many counselors discover early in the counseling enterprise is that no two cases are exactly alike. In general (at bottom, of course) there is only a certain number of fundamental principles and categories that fit all cases (I have discussed this in my pamphlet, *Christ and Your Problems;* but I also said that each situation—in its secondary features—is unique).

I

People who think that they can develop a system, complete with steps and procedures, that neatly fits each and every counseling case will be sadly disappointed in the results of such counseling. The danger of cramming everyone into the same mold doesn't occur only in the over-systematizing attempts of Christians (in my opinion, Chas. Solomon's Spirituotherapy is a good example of this sort of approach) but applies equally as well to reductionist systems like Freudianism, Skinnerianism and Rogerianism. In all of these, people's problems are analyzed and handled according to preconceived human notions of what is wrong (and what to do about that). They do not allow the problem itself to inform the counselor. Instead, the system is pressed down upon the case like a cookie-cutter, and all the facts and data left over are disposed of discreetly (and thereafter ignored). Thus, all problems may be traced back to poor socialization, aggression and sex, to untapped potential in the counselee or to faulty environmental conditioning—depending on whether one's orientation is Freudian, Rogerian or Skinnerian.

"I can see that, but don't Christians do the same thing?"

57

Yes and no. By that I mean (first) that Christians see *one* human cause behind problems—Adam's sin. This sin brought God's judgment upon man and his environment.

"Well, there you are."

Yes, but where are we? Think for a moment, about which system allows for more flexibility. Is it the one that goes back—all the way back—to Adam's sin, as the overarching general cause, or one that finds the source of human problems in some later, secondary, more limited factor? Frankly, I am tired of reading snide remarks by some Christians (and by non-Christians about Christians) to the effect that biblical counseling is inflexible because it sees sin in everything. This is said (knowingly) as if it were obvious that, by acknowledging the Bible's teaching that all men are born corrupt and guilty because of original sin, one limits his ability to counsel. Let me protest loudly, "Not so!"

No one, and I say this advisedly, *no one* limits counseling less than the one who takes human problems back to their beginning.[1] It is those who stop at some point short of this who will limit counseling. They not only limit themselves to a truncated view of man in which all the important data about his creation, fall and the redemption in Christ are ignored, but (as a result) limit their analysis of the human predicament to partial and misunderstood factors. To find the etiology of the human problems that counselors attempt to solve in some less general, later source distorts the picture by limiting it. When a theoretician sees human misery stemming from only one source of human life—the relationship to parents, to authority figures, to the environment, to himself, etc.—he sees reality only in the most limited (and therefore) inflexible way. On the other hand, to find Adam's sin at the fountainhead of human misery is to open *all the possibilities* of examining the place of these resulting effect-cause-effect elements that flow out of Adam's sin. This means that Christians too can see

---

1. Of course, I might go back further to discuss God's sovereignty in the matter, but I am doing this in another book soon to be published. Since going back to Adam's sin takes the Christian back further than any other system, my point is sustained without going still further.

difficulties coming from bad human relationships in all dimensions. But because they see man's difficulty ultimately as the result of a bad relationship to God, they see all these factors as secondary. And they interpret the problem much more *broadly*. Christians will see poor socialization, development of human potential and environmental influence quite differently than Freud, Rogers or Skinner. They will see these as derived, complicating problems; not as basic ones. And, because they see them as deriving their power in man's life from Adam's sin and God's judgment, they will interpret them quite differently; much more broadly. So, it is not the Christian who has narrowed the possibilities; that charge must be laid on the desks of those who fail to acknowledge God's basic problem-solution pattern found in the creation-fall-redemption theme of the Scriptures. A truncated outlook on life is not chargeable to the Christian who has a world view that stretches from eternity past to eternity future. Others *must* (from the denial of the biblical data) absolutize some one factor in human life further on down the chain of events as the cause of problems (and therefore point to a limited solution to them). A wrong analysis (growing out of too limited a view of man's problem) leads to wrong solutions (far less than the larger solution in Christ).

Anyone who limits his understanding of the human predicament by rejecting the biblical analysis is far off base. It is time for this to be said, *widely,* and time for Christians who (ironically, in the name of a "broader" or "enlarged" view) restrict their own counseling by adopting non-Christian presuppositions and methods to hear it too. Christian, burst the bands of non-Christian counseling theory and practice and enter into the full liberty that is in Christ.

II

Christians have a large Bible, and they must learn to exercise all the freedom that their Bible allows. Biblical principles cover *all* of life; they cut a very wide swath. They speak of all the tragedies that develop in divine/human and human/human relationships. All of life in principle (and much in practical example[2]) comes under their purview. Parental and peer influence, child discipline, marriage and family goals and roles, business and work ethic, government, personal ethics, sex, worship—all these—and much more—are subjects discussed in the Scriptures (but differently than anywhere else). How can a Christian, then, help but become a broadly based, widely ranging counselor when his interests are as broad as the Bible?

To limit Christian counseling to some narrow set of rules (or steps) that one has improperly abstracted (and absolutized) from the Bible—as if this were all that God has to say about human living (e.g., "all you have to do is get out of the way and let Christ live His life through you") is to make a travesty out of the true breadth and scope of biblical change.

In another book (soon to be published) I have discussed the wealth of biblical terms that are used to describe the act and the results of human sin. In that place, I consider seventeen distinct words (and that study isn't exhaustive!). True understanding of man's problems and God's solutions, then, is not quite so simple or so limited as some may think (or may misrepresent me as thinking—this is done all the time). The Bible acknowledges the fact that sin was a *great* tragedy; it has an effect on the total man and the totality of his created environment. To fasten counseling to but one (or even two) of these numerous baneful effects (as the cause) is to err by limiting what God has exposed as a vastly larger problem. Sin is the universal, yes; but its effects are numerous and varied.

Therefore, in his analysis of counselee problems, in the solutions that he proposes to them, in the approaches that he takes, the Christian counselor may (must) range throughout the length and breadth of the Bible. It is not enough (1) to isolate one or two biblical passages (or truths) in any exclusive way, or (2) to develop one's own *closed* system from them. To do so, inevitably, is to ignore much that the Scriptures say and teach.

One's systematizing of biblical materials on counseling, of necessity, must be growing and open ended. Qualifying terms ("largely,"

---

2. Cf. Phil. 4:9.

"often," "sometimes," "most," "many," etc.) will appear regularly in much of the writing of those who undertake to systematize the biblical data (I am continually astounded at the way some critics seem to fail to recognize carefully worded qualifications when making their comments). New explorations into the hinterlands of Scripture will continue to be made. Calls for help must be issued. One could study the Bible a lifetime and not begin to exhaust it. That is why his system must be constructed with flexibility. It must be able to admit and assimilate new scriptural discoveries. Counselors will achieve this by *absolutizing only that which the Bible itself absolutizes* (e.g., "You shall not commit adultery").

III

Flexibility of system, therefore, means being as flexible as the Scriptures. Jesus dealt with no two persons in exactly the same way (study His approaches to persons in the Gospel of John.) Counselors, too, must learn to allow their thoughts and plans to flow into varying situations with all the variety and breadth that the Bible affords them.

It certainly would be a tragedy of the first water if someone were to systematize nouthetic counseling too soon and so tightly (narrowly) as to belie its commitment to all of the expansive vistas of the Word. God forbid this to happen!

Rather, let biblical counselors never shut the door to any new truth from the Scriptures. Let us keep our options open to all God has to say. Nouthetic counseling, to be truly biblical, must always be closed to non-Christian thought, but always open to the Bible. Therefore, it must *never* become a closed system.

True to this fact, each counselor ought to expect to discover new facts about counseling all the time—no matter how small some may be. Let him not fear new material—it will never upset what he *truly* holds in accordance with the Scriptures, since the Bible never contradicts itself. Biblical counseling never becomes pat, cut-and-dried, dull; it is always an adventure. Biblical counseling is flexible—and, therefore, exciting!

II

Adaptability in Counseling

Closely connected with the notion of inflexibility (see the previous chapter in this book) is the problem of task-oriented counselors who are more wrapped up in the process of counseling than in helping people.

Take a parallel: Who hasn't sat in a Sunday School class under a teacher whose one goal was to "cover the material" during the allotted time? He will bypass vital questions and concerns, ignore comments, etc., to reach his one-and-only major goal. He will skim important passages, rush through doctrinal complexities, hurdle living issues, all in his mad dash to get to the end of the lesson before the bell rings. He covers the ground all right, but also covers up the truth! Such "teachers" really think little about the people in front of them. They are engaged in an activity labelled "teaching," but that actually would be more accurately called *reaching*. They care only about reaching some arbitrarily chosen point by a specified time. When they do so, they are happy and cut another notch on their Bibles.

Some counselors view their work similarly: There are certain things to be done by a certain session. They will plow ahead at all cost (usually a rather great one), making sure that they get everything done on time. But counseling rarely proceeds uninterruptedly according to schedule. People who have learned to do everything that way will not make good counselors until they relearn biblical adaptability.

While there must be planning, order, direction and even (tentative) scheduling, these all must be adaptable. For instance, one simply may not barrel ahead toward his next counseling goal, giving new homework, when the previous week's homework is yet incomplete. Better to stick to what has been assigned already, discover what got in the way, lay plans for getting it done this time, and reassigning it (perhaps with *one* small, new assignment).

"But this sets counseling back a week!"

Yes, but going on may set it back permanently! If you don't take the time when it is needed, you will allow problems to pile up and defeat you.

When the counselee's agenda differs from the counselor's in any significant way, it is far better to spend one or two weeks (if need be) to discuss this and reach a biblical agreement. Plunging ahead on two different tracks may mean moving fast—but in two different directions!

What I am calling for is genuine adaptability in counseling. But of what does adaptability consist? Quite contrary to what some fear, the first, and most basic element, in true adaptability is order and structure. I have known people who, when I speak of adaptability, shudder because they think immediately of confusion and chaos. Exactly the opposite is the case. The disorganized person, with *no goals,* doesn't know how to bring about desired results because he has no plan or program for doing so. He may be unpredictable, but he is not adaptive. *There must be a plan to be adaptive.*

It is only when both his long and short range goals and objectives are clear (when a counselor knows basically where he wants to go and how to get there) that he can adapt those ways and means to changing and unpredictable circumstances that occur in God's providence. Counselors, to be biblical, must allow for God's surprises!

In other words, to be adaptive, one must have something to adapt! The two Latin words behind our compound word *adapt* say it all; they are "fit to." We *fit* our counseling plans *to* unknown and unexpected turns of events when we adapt. An adaptive counselor is always busy fitting things to providential events.

But there is also a second essential ingredient in adaptability: *willingness to bend.* Some counselors fail, not from lack of basic ability, but from *unwillingness.* This quality is important. Bending is not always pleasant. When one has put together a shiny, nice, airtight plan, it isn't always easy to scrap it (or radically modify it). Sometimes, like the teacher mentioned above, the counselor finds it hard to adapt his schedule. Some counselors are so enamored with their plans and programs, that they won't bend. But it doesn't matter how good the program is on paper, if it doesn't *fit to* a changed situation, or if the counselee isn't moving at the pace proposed, the program (in the end) is really worthless. The only way to save all the work that went into it, and at the same time to truly help the counselee, is to *adapt* it.

I must distinguish between *adaptation* and *accommodation;* there is no real similarity between the two. Indeed, they must be viewed as processes that are antithetical to one another. The former takes place *always within the boundaries of biblical principle;* the latter does not. Adaptation is fitting *that which is essentially the same* to *a changing situation;* accommodation is *reshaping* one's views, etc., to fit the situation (which itself may not have changed at all).

Christian counselors must not accommodate biblical truths and requirements to the counselee's sinful life or desires. While a counselor *himself* may have to bend (in ways often inconvenient and unpleasant to him), he may not accommodate God's Word. His timetable may have to be rewritten, but he must still insist on repentance and forgiveness. When, in a case like that, where repentance is necessary as a foundation for all that follows, the counselor dare not move on until repentance takes place (to do otherwise would be to compromise the absoluteness of God's requirement.) But he must not *force* repentance either (people who do so, often have a Bible-notching mentality and do not adjust their own schedules well). Adaptation, in a case like this, means willingness to wait.

Take another situation. A counselee finds it more difficult to curb his anger than he ought to, given the amount of time and effort expended on the problem. Adaptability says, "Well, by now I had planned to be well on my way to doing X, Y and Z. Here I am, stuck with this problem. Is it a problem that must be solved before moving to something else? In some cases it is (so you wait and work); in some cases it isn't. What I'll do, then, is rearrange items I intended to handle in sequence so that *while continuing to work on anger,* I shall begin also to work on X and perhaps even Y." The *order* of the plan has been adapted; the *goals* have not. Accommodation would bypass the anger question and go on to something else, thereby indicating (wittingly or unwittingly) that God's requirements about anger (and who knows what else) are negotiable.

The fundamental difference, then, between adaptation and accommodation is clear: The former tailors human plans so as to accomplish God's desires; the latter ignores God's requirements in order to satisfy human desires.

A counselor who has never learned how to adapt will fail continually.

"But, how does one learn to be adaptable? They didn't teach that in seminary."

Perhaps they should have; it is an important matter. If I were teaching counselors in a classroom situation, I would do something like this:

1. Choose ten counseling situations from *The Christian Counselor's Casebook.*

2. One by one, through the first five, have students draw up a counseling plan for the next counseling session (or for the remainder of the one sketched in the *Casebook*), setting forth basic goals:

   a. Goals for the session;

   b. Areas for discussion and decision;

   c. Ways and means for achieving these goals in terms of concrete homework assignments.

3. Then, I would have them introduce five possible hindrances (changes, unforeseen developments, etc.) that might arise to impede counseling as projected.

4. And, finally, I would have them lay out five alternative plans (one for each of the five cases) for attaining these goals.

5. Then, I'd have them do the same as homework for the remaining five cases.[1]

In other words, what a counselor needs to learn is that there is more than one biblically legitimate way to enter the same house (try *all* doors, windows, chimney, etc.). Don't adapt goals, but whatever may be changed *without departing from biblical standards* may be adapted.

---

1. Of course these procedures could also be role-played.

12

Reminding

There is a great deal of first-time instruction that must be done by counselors since a number of counselees seem to be utterly ignorant even of many of the basic scriptural principles of living as well as the truths that pertain to particular situations and issues that arise. Since sin tends to draw people away from the study and personal application of the Word, and since Christians have been brainwashed into thinking they must have "psychology for living" and not just the Bible for living (how did Jesus and the church get along with just the Bible for 1900 years?!), it is necessary to do much educating in counseling sessions.

But while that is true, it is not all. There are many things that people know pretty well—the only problem is that they are not doing them.[1] What they need is not further instruction, or, in some cases, not even how-to information (though many desperately need this most of all), but a powerful *reminder*.

That is why Paul urges Titus to *"Remind* them . . ." (Tit. 3:1), and tells Timothy to *"Remind* them about these things. . . ." That is why Peter wrote, "I shall not neglect to *remind* you continually about these things even though you are established in the truth about which I am now writing" (II Pet. 1:12), and continues, saying, "I think it is right as long as I am in this tent to stir you up by *reminding* you" (1:13), and concludes, "I also shall do everything I can to make it possible for you to *remember* these things after my departure" (II Pet. 1:15). The risen Jesus calls upon the church at Sardis to *"Remember* . . . what you have received and heard; keep it and repent" (Rev. 3:3), and He tells the church in Ephesus: *"Remember,* then, the place from which you have fallen; repent and do the deeds

---

1. Cf. Phil. 3:16.

that you did at first" (Rev. 2:5).[2]

From these several selected passages it is clear that remembering is an important part of Christian growth, a significant factor in bringing about change and a powerful incentive to live differently. In a variety of situations, therefore, the Christian counselor must call his counselees to remembrance, often even spelling out for them once again *what to remember and how.*

From just these few passages, we may learn something about *what* it is that a Christian must remember, and in what sort of circumstances a counselor may find it important to remind him of these things.

1. Clearly, it is of prime importance that one call to memory truths one has already been taught which he needs to remember, so that he may live by them. The *Lord's* supper is this kind of reminder. Both in his letter to Titus and in his letters to Timothy, Paul urges the good minister of Jesus Christ to remind the members of Christ's church about Christian teaching, so that they may, by applying this, "learn to engage in good deeds."

2. But that is not all. Especially in the Titus passage, Paul seems to indicate that Christians need to be reminded of the past life from which God graciously redeemed them, both to contrast their present state with it and to urge them to progress beyond it (cf. Tit. 3:3-8). Peter makes this point clearly when he speaks of those who have *"forgotten* the cleansing" of their past sins (II Pet. 1:9; often, the negative side of remembering is stressed; cf. Heb. 13:16). And even when no direct *call to remember* is given (as such), Paul (and others) follow the practice of reminding believers about the past from which they were rescued (cf. Eph. 2:1-3; the whole book of Hebrews is such a reminder). So there is a second reason.

3. In the two Revelation passages quoted above, the reminder is hooked to repentance (incidentally, note how *Christians* are

---

2. See also Deut. 1:29ff.; 6:12ff.; 7:18ff.; 8:2, 11, 14, 18, 19; 9:7, etc.

called to repentance in contrast to some current trends in counseling circles that deny the need to do so). What could better bring repentance than to contrast present sinful living with "what you have received and heard," and (even more powerful, in some ways) "the place from which you have fallen"? In these instances the doctrine not only had been *taught,* the teaching also had been "received" (i.e., understood and accepted as trustworthy and authoritative). Receiving Christian teaching that way involves a plain commitment on the part of the one who receives it to live by it. And if one had once walked in the truth, but left it, he needed to be reminded of his first love and first works.

4. Lastly, but not altogether separated from what has been mentioned already, Peter says that he reminds his readers, even though what he had to say was well established among them as truth (i.e., "received"), in order *to stir them up.* Reminders, appropriately given at the right place and time (that is what distinguishes them from nagging) are powerful motivators. Counselors are always seeking ways to *motivate* counselees; let Peter teach you one (learn also from Paul and the writer of Hebrews. On this, see "Motivation in Hebrews," in *Matters of Concern,* pp. 28ff.). The verb Peter uses, translated "stir up" is a strong one, indicating action that gets results. It is used, for instance, of *awakening* someone from sleep (not just trying to), of a calm sea becoming *aroused* in a storm, etc. Peter reminds his readers in order to wake them up.

But reminders must be of such a sort, given in such a way, at such a time as is appropriate, or they may tend to do the opposite. A time of need (the time that counselors usually come into contact with counselees) is an especially appropriate time for reminders. But even then they must be given helpfully; not in an "I told you so" manner.

All in all, then, reminding can be an extraordinarily effective tool in the hands of counselors. I probably didn't really have to write this chapter to most of you to tell you something new; I just wanted to stir you up by way of reminders!

13

A Basic Christian Vocabulary
Compiled by Jay E. Adams

I have discovered that in the field of counseling many persons know more about psychological terms than they know about Christian vocabulary. That is tragic. I have, therefore, determined to do something about this lack.

Every field of learning has its specialized vocabulary. In order to read and understand the literature connected with it and form accurate concepts, you must master the basic vocabulary of the field. From one viewpoint, it is possible to say that a person "knows" his subject in direct proportion to his ability to be at home with its vocabulary. While learning vocabulary meanings does not necessarily mean comprehending, believing or applying to life the ideas behind them, it surely aids. Ideas cannot be *accurately* formed apart from such understanding. And it is difficult to live what you don't understand. Nowhere is it more important to be familiar with terminology than in the greatest of all fields of study—Christianity. And within the broad scope of Christianity, there is great need among Christian counselors for just such an understanding.

The vocabulary is also published separately in pamphlet form for distribution in quantity.*

This list is entirely basic. It is what every Christian should know as a *minimum*. Other words, or fuller explanations of some of these may be looked up in a good Bible dictionary or systematic theology text. A planned study of the terms in this list will help you to become

---

* Copies may be obtained from the publisher or from CCEF (latter's address on page 41).

familiar with these words. Learn a word each day. Look up several verses in your concordance that use the biblical word. Use it in conversation at least three times during the day. Go over all the past words that you have already learned. Knowing these terms will help you to become conversant with the Scriptures and the best Christian literature.

Adoption—One of the figures of speech used to describe the reception of believers into the family of God (Gal. 4:5; Eph. 1:4). It emphasizes especially the fact that men are not naturally born the children of God. All the rights and privileges of sonship pertain to an adopted child.

Advent—A coming or appearance; used of the first (II Pet. 1:16) and second comings of Christ.

Agnostic—Literally, "he who does not know." Agnostics are doubters of two kinds: honest doubters (seekers who are troubled by their agnosticism and who want to know the truth if possible); dishonest doubters (who have stopped searching for truth, concluding that ultimate knowledge is impossible).

Altar—A place of sacrifice. True Christian churches do not have altars today because Calvary was the last sacrifice acceptable to God (cf. Heb. 9–10).

Amen—A response denoting consent or agreement and meaning, literally, "so be it." It may be spoken sincerely, reverently and audibly at the close of prayer (I Cor. 14:16).

Angel—A created spirit (Heb. 1:19) whose name means "messenger" and who is appointed to minister to Christians. Fallen angels are the demons of Scripture (Matt. 25:41). Angels appear in the form of men (Heb. 13:2; Acts 1:10). Humans who die do not become angels, as has been erroneously taught; they are of a separate order of beings (Ps. 8:4-5).

Apocrypha—Uninspired books written during the interval between the writing of the Old and New Testament books. They never were accepted by the Hebrews, Christ, the apostles or the early church. Some of them are wrongly attributed to writers who did not compose them. They contain much interesting history, but also many errors of fact, doctrine, history, and science. It was not until April 8, 1546, that the Roman church declared them to be canonical.

Apologetics—The defense of the Christian faith. The word originally meant a defense made in a law court, and has nothing to do with apologizing.

Apostasy—That state into which those who turn away from the truth enter after they have renounced the faith that they once professed. True Christians never turn apostate. Apostates were not Christians in the first place (I John 2:19; Matt. 7:23).

Apostle—Literally, "one sent forth." The word is used in a general sense of any missionary (cf. Acts 13:3; 14:4, 14), but most frequently in a restricted sense of the twelve men whom Jesus appointed and sent forth to found the church. Their work was foundational (Eph. 2:20; 3:5) and not to be duplicated by others.

Ark—A chest or box. Refers to three things in Scripture: Noah's ark, the boat that looked like a big box; Moses' ark in which he was afloat on the Nile; the ark of the covenant—literally, a box that contained the tables of the Ten Commandments and other valuable items, and was kept in the holy of holies beneath the place where God's presence dwelt.

Assurance—The biblical doctrine that when one is saved, he may *know* it (I John 5:13). God did not want us to guess about our saving relationship to Him.

Atheist—One who does not believe in the existence of God. No person knows enough to be an atheist. He would have to be everywhere at the same time to declare that God is nowhere. If he were, he wouldn't say so—he would be God.

Atonement—The word is used both to denote the satisfaction that is brought about by the death of Christ (issuing in the reconciliation of God and His people), and the death itself which produces the at-one-ment. Christ's atonement was designed for specific persons (John 17:7; Isa. 53:8; Matt. 1:21; etc.). If Christ suffered for the sins of "mankind" in the abstract, He would not be a *personal* Savior and no one could suffer in hell; God would be unjust in exacting the same punishment twice.

Baptism—There are two aspects of baptism. The first is the inward, invisible baptism of the Holy Spirit that occurs at conversion. This is necessary for salvation (Rom. 8:9). The second aspect is outward, visible, water baptism, which symbolizes the inward reality. Water baptism was always performed by sprinkling or pouring, as this alone could adequately symbolize the descent of the Holy Spirit, who is poured out (or shed) upon us. Holy Spirit baptism produces two effects: cleansing (negative) and union with the body of Christ (positive).

Bible—A word that means "book." Since ancient writing paper (papyrus) came from the Mediterranean city of Biblos, the word *biblos* (bible) came to mean "book." The Bible is THE Book. Though written by many authors, God, the Holy Spirit, is the one Author behind them all. Hence, it is rightly viewed as one coherent Book.

Bishop—Literally, "overseer, supervisor or superintendent" (see **Elder**).

Call—There are two calls—the external call (which comes to saved and unsaved alike), i.e., the preaching of the gospel, and the internal (or effectual) call, which is the work of the Holy Spirit in the heart of God's people that regenerates and enables them to believe the gospel. This latter is irresistible.

Calvinism—That scriptural system of theology especially formulated by John Calvin which is founded upon the two basic doctrines of the sovereignty of God and grace.

Christ—The Greek equivalent of the Hebrew word "Messiah," both of which mean the "Anointed One." Jesus was anointed prophet, priest, and king, and this anointing probably took place at His baptism (as there is no other record of an anointing) when the Holy Spirit came upon Him (in John 2:20, 27, the Holy Spirit is called an anointing). The baptism symbolized the anointing of the Holy Spirit (cf. Luke 4:18).

Church—(see **Ecclesiology**).

Commentaries—Volumes supplying background material and interpretations of the verses of various books of the Bible.

Concordance—A book containing all (or nearly all) the words of the Bible listed alphabetically, along with every occurrence of them (by verse). It is valuable for word, doctrinal, or topical studies, the determination of the exact location of half-remembered verses, and many other uses.

Conversion—An "about face." When one has been walking the wrong way, God turns him around in the other direction by regeneration, repentance and faith.

Covenant—An agreement between two or more persons, usually sealed by a bloody sacrifice (hence, one literally "cuts" a covenant). The old and new covenants are to be distinguished from the books that contain them (and bear their name). The covenant of grace is God's plan of salvation, in which He saves men in all eras by grace alone.

Creation—To create is to produce something out of nothing (ex nihilo) Men "make" (i.e., use previously existing materials); God alone can create. In creation, matter was brought into existence.

Deacon—Ordained officers of the church of Christ (Acts 6:6), whose basic function is to take over all temporal matters assigned to them by the elders, are called deacons. Their qualifications are found in I Timothy 3:8-12. Their minimum duties are to visit the sick, care for the poor, and comfort those in trial.

Death—(see **Life**). The separation of the soul (or spirit) from the body (II Cor. 5:8; James 2:26). Spiritual death (Eph. 2) is separation from God in this life. The "second death" (Rev. 20) is the separation of the soul and body from God forever.

Demons—Fallen angels. They are capable of possessing the unsaved, and are to be distinguished in such activity from sickness and madness (which, however, they may cause). The recently proven fact of hypnotism (in which the mind of another can influence the words, thoughts, and actions of a subject) has removed most of the old objections and prejudices against the possibility of demon possession. Many modern notions about demons and their activities are unscriptural.

Depravity, total—The Scriptures teach that men are all together

74

sinful, and individually, altogether sinful (Rom. 3:23; 8:7-8; et al.). Every part of human life has been affected by sin, but not as badly as it might be were it not for God's restraining grace.

Devil (or Satan)—These two words mean "slanderer" and "adversary" respectively, and signify something of the activity of this being. The devil is a fallen angel who is the chief opponent of God and His people. He is not to be conceived of as a horrid-looking creature in red tights, with a pointed tail and horns. Rather, as a spirit, he makes his appearance in many forms, even as an angel of *light* (II Cor. 11:14). Neither does he "run" hell, but shall in the last times be committed to eternal punishment there (Matt. 25:41).

Disciple—A "learner" or "pupil." Discipleship is the biblical method for training and consists of teaching by both word and example.

Discipline—Church discipline is the watchful care over members of Christ's church in an attempt to lead them away from sinful beliefs and practices. It indicates regularity and order in the personal life as well.

Doctrine—"Teaching." The summarized teaching of all the verses of the Bible on any subject is the biblical doctrine (or teaching) on that subject.

Ecclesiology—The study of the church. The word "church" is derived from *ecclesia,* which means, "the called out ones." In Scripture, this term is used to denote two things: (1) The invisible church —all those of every era who have been saved throughout all the world. (2) The visible church—local congregations or groups of them in a particular area; i.e., all those who have been baptized into the fellowship of the organized body. All who are in the visible church are not necessarily in the invisible. Membership in the visible church is not essential for salvation, though membership in the invisible church is. The word "church" is never used in the Bible to denote buildings or denominations (the two uses are definitely modern). The word always refers to people.

Eden—"Pleasures." The phrase "the garden of eden," when literally translated, is "the park of pleasures."

Edification—The building up (or strengthening) of fellow Christians in their faith.

Elder—"Old, or mature man." The Greek is "presbyter" (hence the word "presbyterian" or rule by presbyters). See Titus 1:5-9; I Timothy 3:1-7, et al., for functions and qualifications of the office. The Scripture distinguishes between the ruling elder and the teaching-and-ruling elder (I Tim. 5:17). The latter is also called the pastor and teacher (Eph. 4:11). The word "bishop" (overseer) speaks of the work of the elder, whereas "presbyter" speaks of his qualifications. The presbyter and bishop are the same man (and not two different offices); see Titus 1:5, 7.

Elect—The elect is that company of human beings whom God selected from all eternity to be His people. This election is unconditional, based solely upon His own wise purpose, and in no sense dependent upon the merits or faith of the elect (which are the result and not the cause of election). See Romans 11:7, 28; I Thessalonians 1:4; I Timothy 5:21; Romans 9:11ff.

Epistle—A letter.

Eschatology—The study of the last things. The doctrines concerning the second coming of Christ, the resurrection, the judgment and the final state of man.

Eternal security—The scriptural teaching that a man once saved can never be lost (cf. I Pet. 1:3-5; Rom. 8:35-39; John 17:12; 10:28-29; Phil. 1:6; II Tim. 1:12). To teach that a saved man could be lost is to admit that God is not a good Father, Christ's work on the cross can be frustrated by Satan, and that God fails to keep His promises. One continues in the faith by perseverance. God enables true believers to continue.

Evangelism—The presentation of the gospel message for the purpose of leading others to saving faith in Christ. See **Gospel.**

Faith—Trust, dependence, reliance, belief. Saving faith consists of knowledge, assent, and trust. When directed toward an unworthy object, faith becomes gullibility.

Fasting—To abstain from food, either partially or wholly, for the purpose of mourning; to allow time for prayer; in case of national emergencies or prior to undertaking an important task. Biblical fasting must be voluntary and occasional; not stated.

Flesh—Besides its ordinary meaning, this word often has the special biblical meaning of the body habituated to evil (see esp. Rom. 6–8; Gal. 5).

Gehenna—(see **Hades**).

Gifts—Abilities given by God to His people for His service and their edification.

Glorification—The divinely wrought change that takes place in the believer when he dies, whereby he becomes sinless (and especially referring to the resurrection, when he will be made complete in perfection of both body and soul).

Gospel—Literally, "good news." This good news, which must be believed for salvation, consists of two elements: (1) The penal, substitutionary death of Christ for our sins; (2) The bodily resurrection of Christ (cf. I Cor. 15:1, 3, 4).

Grace—The unmerited favor of God shown toward men. The unearned love and mercy God shows toward persons who deserve the opposite. *Common grace* is the good which God does for believers and unbelievers alike (Matt. 5:45), while *special grace* is the salvation and consequent blessings He dispenses to the elect alone. The word is used also to designate *help* or *aid* that God gives to His children.

Guilt—Culpability before God or man, making one liable to punishment. This word should *never* be confused (as it so often is in counseling circles) with having a sense (or feeling) of guilt.

Hades—Literally, "the unseen world" (i.e., the invisible world; unfortunately translated "hell" in the KJ version). This is the general biblical word for the world of departed spirits. It corresponds to the Hebrew "sheol." Hades is composed of at least two areas: (1) The place of bliss (Abraham's bosom, paradise, heaven). (2) The place of punishment (gehenna, hell, the lake of fire, the place of torment). The word gehenna is properly translated "hell" in the modern sense of the word as the place of eternal punishment.

Heart—The inner life one lives before God and himself. Not equated with feelings (as in our day).

Heaven—There are three heavens (cf. II Cor. 12:1-4). They are: the atmosphere (or air) surrounding the earth, the sky (space, where the stars and planets are located), and the third heaven (where God dwells).

Hell—(see **Hades**).

Heresy—Teaching contrary to the Word of God that denies the way of salvation. The word originally referred to schismatic activity. The two concepts are related.

Holy—The word refers to any person or thing which has been separated, or "set apart" from sin (or regular use) unto God (or special use). In many places, it can mean simply *special*.

Holy Spirit—The third Person of the Trinity. He dwells within every true believer.

Idolatry—The love and worship of any substitute for the true God, whether a physical idol, a person, or a possession (cf. Col. 3:5b).

Impute—To reckon or account, as in Romans 4:6, 11, 22, where righteousness is reckoned to one's account by faith.

Incarnation—The act of Christ becoming a human being by assuming flesh. Christ was true man (in every sense apart from sin) as well as true God.

Inspiration—Literally, that which is "god-breathed." The Scriptures were inspired of God in such a way as to render them inerrant and infallible in language as well as thought. Inspiration refers to the writing, not to the writers.

Intermediate state—The conscious state of the soul (spirit) between death and the final resurrection.

Jehovah—An improper spelling of the Hebrew name for God, which is, literally, Yahveh. Yahveh comes from the verb to be, and means "The One who Is" (cf. Ex. 3:14).

Jesus—Means "Jehovah is salvation." It is the N.T. form of the O.T. name Joshua. It speaks clearly of Christ's mission as Saviour (cf. Matt. 1:12).

Jew—A term derived from "Judah," meaning "one who belongs to the tribe of Judah." This word is used only after the exile and restoration. Judah was the principal tribe to return, but the designation embraces all who returned to the land, whether of Judah or another tribe. In the N.T., Paul broadens its usage still more, as he changes it from a racial to a religious term which includes all true Christians (Rom. 2:28, 29).

Justification—A legal action whereby the believing sinner is forgiven, cleared of all his sins, and accounted righteous on the books of heaven. Justification is by faith alone (Rom. 4).

Law—A term used broadly to refer to the whole Bible, the O.T. Scriptures, and more specifically to the Pentateuch (the first five books of the O.T.), and in its most restricted sense, to the Ten Commandments alone.

Liberalism—That system which, because of disbelief in the inerrancy and infallibility of the Bible, is led to reject the doctrines and teachings contained therein. It is unbelief parading under the name of Christianity. In its more recent form, it attempts to distinguish the Word of God (which is said to be found behind the words of the Bible) from the Bible itself. The Word of God is said to be true and perfect, but the Bible imperfect. Liberalism, in all its forms, always challenges God's Word.

Life—The Bible speaks of three kinds of life (and death, q.v.):

Life (union)		**Death** (separation)
Physical	Body + Soul	Body – Soul
Spiritual	Soul + God	Soul – God
Eternal	Body and Soul + God	Body and Soul – God

Lord's Day—The first day of the week, on which the Christian church is to worship (cf. Rev. 1:10). Whereas the seventh-day Sabbath was a day of total physical rest, the Lord's Day is to be one of total spiritual activity. These elements of the Sabbath and the Lord's Day are not to be confounded.

Love—Constructive good will. The highest gift of God. Not a matter of emotions first, but of giving to another what God commands, out of obedience to Him.

Messiah—(see **Christ**).

Miracle—A powerful work of God in which He, acting directly and not through natural means (as in Providence, q.v.), steps into the stream of history and time, to supersede natural laws by supernatural ones.

Monotheism—Belief in one God. Christians are monotheists (who believe in one God in three Persons) but not unitarians (who believe in one god who is but one person).

Mystery—Not some incomprehensible truth, but that which God has hidden until the appointed time for it to be revealed (Rom. 16: 25-26).

Omnipotence—The power of God, which is unlimited. God is all-powerful and can do anything He wants to do. He cannot (and, of course, does not wish to) do anything contrary to Himself.

Omnipresence—The ability of God to be everywhere at the same time. God alone is omnipresent. Some persons speak (erroneously) as if Satan were too.

Omniscience—God's all-comprehensive knowledge of every past, present, and future event.

Original sin—The doctrine of Scripture that states that humans are born sinners (cf. Ps. 51:5; 58:3; Prov. 22:15; Gen. 8:21; Eph. 2:3). Proof that infants are sinners from the earliest age is found in the fact that they are subject to death, and the wages of SIN is death (Rom. 6:23).

Orthodoxy—Literally, "straight opinion or thought." Orthodoxy is conformity to historical biblical Christianity.

Pantheism—The belief that the universe is god. Examples: Christian Science, Unity.

Passover—One of the three annual festivals of the Jews, which commemorates the deliverance from Egypt, and especially the accompanying plague upon the firstborn (cf. Ex. 12).

Perfectionism—Sinless perfection. Though set forth as the Christian's goal (Matt. 5:4-8), it is an impossibility in this life because of sinful human nature. Those who claim such perfection, John says (I John 1:8-10), deceive themselves (by representing sin not to be sin), do not possess the truth, make God a liar (this false doctrine is a very serious heresy), and do not have the Word of God in them.

Perseverance—(see **Eternal security**).

Polytheism—Belief in many gods. Examples: paganism (Roman and Greek religion), Mormonism.

Prayer—Simply talking with God. There are four kinds of prayer: adoration, confession, thanksgiving, and supplication (ACTS).

Preaching—The communication of biblical truth through human personality to change human beings.

Predestination—The scriptural teaching that from all eternity God has planned everything that happens (cf. Eph. 1:11; Rom. 8:29, etc.).

Priest—One who offers sacrifices, and who stands between man and God as a mediator. Today, there is no need for a special priesthood, since all Christians are priests, offering spiritual sacrifices of thanksgiving and praise (cf. I Pet. 2:5).

Prophet—One who *forth*tells the word of God; a preacher. Most of the inspired prophets also had the power to *fore*tell the future.

Providence—God's superintending and ordering of all events through natural means so as to infallibly work out His purposes in history. Sometimes the word is used to refer only to God's benevolent acts toward Christians.

Redemption—The purchasing (or buying back) of God's people at the cost of Christ's sufferings and death. The price is not paid to Satan, but to God. Salvation brings *more* than redemption since (in Christ) man has been raised to God's throne in the heavenlies.

Reformed—The system of doctrine stemming from the Reformation that includes Calvinism (q.v.), presbyterian government, and covenant theology.

Regeneration—A new birth, brought about through the implantation of spiritual life by the Holy Spirit.

Repentance—To repent means to "change one's mind." True repentance is, therefore, a thorough change of outlook with reference to God, Christ, and one's self. It leads to a change of life. It is not necessarily connected with great emotional experiences.

Resurrection—The raising of a body from the grave in order to reunite it to its non-body part (spirit).

Revelation—An "unveiling." The Bible is God's revelation to us of the facts we need to know about Himself, the universe, and ourselves. God has revealed truth through creation (general revelation) and through the Bible (special revelation). The former is insufficient to lead to salvation, though adequate to lead to condemnation. This necessitates the latter. The former can be interpreted correctly only by means of the latter.

Righteousness—Rightness in God's sight. The only righteousness acceptable to God is that which He Himself reckons to us through faith. All self-righteousness is condemned (cf. Rom. 10:2-4; Tit. 3:5, et al.).

Saints—"Set apart or holy (q.v.) ones." All Christians are saints while yet alive, even though far from perfect (I Cor. 1:2; Rom. 1:7).

Salvation—Rescue from a desperate situation; specifically, from condemnation in hell (q.v.). Our salvation may be fully described in three tenses:

Past—we HAVE BEEN SAVED from the penalty of sin = justification.

Present—we ARE BEING SAVED from the power of sin = sanctification.

Prospective—we SHALL BE SAVED from the presence of sin = glorification.

Satan—(see **Devil**).

Sanctification—"Separation, setting apart" (from the same root as "holy" and "saint," q.v.). The gradual *process* whereby the believer is set apart more and more from sin to God is called sanctification. It covers the entire earthly lifespan from justification to glorification, and is not to be thought of as an *act* (like justification). Counseling is part of the process of sanctification, by which one puts off the old person and puts on the new person.

Separation—The Christian is to be distinct and different from the unsaved. He is to have no close ties of fellowship with them socially or ecclesiastically (cf. II Cor. 6:14-18).

Sin—Disobedience to the law of God, manifested by doing that which is forbidden or failure to do that which is commanded. At bottom sin is disobedience to God. While it has a horizontal dimension, sin must be viewed essentially vertically as (above all else) an affront against God.

Soteriology—The study of the doctrine (biblical teaching) of salvation.

Soul—The same as the spirit but with a different shade of meaning. The soul is a spirit viewed as united with a body, while a spirit is a soul viewed as disembodied.

Spirit—(see **Soul**). A person without a body.

Temptation—Seduction to sin. Men are tempted by the world system, the flesh (their own sinful habits and desires), and the devil. Temptation is not sin; yielding to it is.

Testimony—The witness (good or bad) that the life and words of a Christian bear toward the unsaved, especially concerning the way of salvation and the truth of the Christian faith.

Theism—Belief in a personal God. Christian theism is belief in the true God.

Theology—The study and systematic formulation of scriptural doctrine (q.v.).

Tongue—A language (cf. Acts 2). As a sign to unbelievers, to attest to one's apostleship (II Cor. 12:12) and his call to write Scripture (Heb. 2:4); a means for the conversion of the lost. In the early days of the church God gave some Christians the ability to speak in foreign languages without learning them. Regulations for the use of this gift may be found in I Corinthians 14.

Trinity—The word refers to one God, who is three Persons: Father, Son, Spirit. Christians do not believe in three Gods.

Unitarianism—The belief that God is but one Person; a denial of the Christian doctrine of the Trinity.

Version—A translation of the Scriptures. No versions are inspired; only the original writings were.

Vicarious—Substitutionary. Christ became the Substitute for His people on the cross, bearing the punishment for their sins.

Virgin birth—This is the miracle by which the Holy Spirit effected the

83

incarnation (q.v.) without ordinary natural means. It assured both the sinlessness of Christ and His two natures.

Worship—The respect and honor which one shows to that thing or Person which he considers divine (or uppermost in life).

Wrath—The just judgment and vengeance of God upon those who persist in sin and do not accept His offer of salvation.

These definitions are brief, because of the nature of this work. My hope, however, is that this list will provide a handy ready-reference for the Christian, and that he will spend time studying it in the fashion described at the beginning.

Index of Scripture References

II Corinthians
11:23-29 — 20
12:1-4 — 78
12:12 — 83

Galatians
4:5 — 71
4:9 — 37

Ephesians
1:4 — 71
1:11 — 81
2:1-3 — 68
2:3 — 80
4:11 — 76
4:17 — 15
4:26-32 — 20

Philippians
1 — 20
1:16 — 76
3:16 — 67
4 — 5

Colossians
3:5b — 78

I Thessalonians
1:4 — 76

I Timothy
3:1-7 — 76
3:8-12 — 74
5:21 — 76

II Timothy
1:12 — 76

II Timothy
4:7 — 39

Titus
1:5-9 — 76
3:1 — 67
3:5 — 82
3:3-8 — 68

Hebrews
1:19 — 72
2:4 — 83
9, 10 — 72
12:15-17 — 14
13:2 — 71
13:16 — 68

James
2:26 — 74

I Peter
1:3-5 — 76
2:5 — 81

II Peter
1:9 — 68
1:12-15 — 67
1:16 — 72

I John
2:19 — 72
5:13 — 72

Revelation
1:10 — 79
2:5 — 68, 69
3:3 — 67, 68

Index of Subjects

Index of Persons